DORIS GRUMBACH is one of this country's most distinguished novelists and critics. Her novels include *Chamber Music, The Missing Person, The Ladies,* and *The Magician's Girl,* all of which are soon to be available in Norton paperback editions, as is her memoir *Coming into the End Zone.* She was previously the literary editor of *The New Republic* and has been a regular book reviewer for National Public Radio. She lives in Sargentville, Maine.

BY DORIS GRUMBACH
IN NORTON PAPERBACK

Chamber Music
Coming into the End Zone
The Missing Person

COMING INTO

THE END ZONE

A Memoir

DORIS GRUMBACH

W · W · NORTON & COMPANY

New York   London

Excerpt from "Women" from The Blue Estuaries by Louise Bogan. Copyright
© 1986 by Louise Bogan. Reprinted by permission of Farrar, Straus & Giroux.
Excerpt from "Here Lies" from Collected Poems of Stevie Smith. Copyright
© 1972 by Stevie Smith. Reprinted by permission of New Directions Publishing
Corporation. Excerpt from "The Critic" from The Collected Poems of Frank
O'Hara. Copyright © 1981 by Maureen Granville-Smith, Administratrix of the
Estate of Frank O'Hara. Reprinted by permission of Alfred A. Knopf, Inc.
Excerpt from "Ash Wednesday" in Collected Poems, 1909–1962 by T. S.
Eliot, copyright 1936 by Harcourt Brace Jovanovich, Inc., copyright © 1964, 1963
by T. S. Eliot, reprinted by permission of the publisher. Excerpt from "Little
Gidding" in Four Quartets, copyright 1943 by T. S. Eliot and renewed 1971 by
Esme Valerie Eliot, reprinted by permission of Harcourt Brace Jovanovich, Inc.

The text of this book is composed in Bembo,
with the display set in Cochin Italic.
Composition and manufacturing by the Haddon Craftsmen, Inc.
Book design by Jack Meserole.

First published as a Norton paperback 1993.

Library of Congress Cataloging-in-Publication Data
Grumbach, Doris.
      Coming into the end zone / by Doris Grumbach.
      p. cm.
      1. Grumbach, Doris—Diaries. 2. Novelists, American—20th
century—Diaries. I. Title.
PS3557.R83Z462 1991
818'.5403—dc20
[B]   90-27187

ISBN 0-393-30944-4

W.W. Norton & Company, Inc., 500 Fifth Avenue, New York, N.Y. 10110

W.W. Norton & Company Ltd, 10 Coptic Street, London WC1A 1PU

    4   5   6   7   8   9   0

THIS MEMOIR IS FOR

ISAAC WHEELER

AND

MAYA YAROWSKY

MY PERSONAL REPRESENTATIVES

IN THE FUTURE

*Now this is not the end. It is
not even the beginning of the end.
But it is, perhaps, the end of the
beginning.*

—WINSTON CHURCHILL

*I*t is eccentric and inaccurate to claim that the July of my seventieth birthday is a landmark in my life. Surely there were other important Julys scattered throughout those many years. For instance, that month of my fifth year when I realized I had to go to school in September. It was a prospect I dreaded, believing in my heart that I was already sufficiently educated by Central Park, by the books I had read since I was three and a half, and by the disruptive arrival that year of a baby sister who taught me terrible lessons in displacement, resentment, hatred.

In the July of my twentieth year after I had graduated from college I ignored the event because I was in a state of shock. During the May that preceded it, my friend and classmate John Ricksecker had jumped from the roof of the School of Commerce at New York University, ending his troubled life and my innocence about how good life was and how hopeful our future. It was May 1939, a few months before Hitler marched into Poland. Was he determined not to be made to go to war? I never knew why he chose to jump, or whether he did.

For he said as he was dying that he 'climbed up and fell.' I have always mourned him and felt responsible for his death. As a woman not liable to be 'called up,' I was overwhelmed by the unfairness of the draft, making me realize the destructive power of sexual inequities and the injustice of death.

There was the July two years later after I married in May. I began to see that legal unions did not solve problems of inner turmoil and loneliness. . . . The Julys in my middle years after two of my children were born and I began to have serious doubts about my capacity for motherhood. The July I lay in bed in a tiny room in a country house, afflicted with viral pneumonia, listening to the sounds of husband and children downstairs, and wondering how to escape from everything and everyone I knew.

My sixtieth July was terrible. I remembered, as though I had been struck a blow, that my mother had died at fifty-nine. Somehow, to have exceeded her life span by a year seemed to me a terrible betrayal. It was worse than the guilt that choked me later at the thought of having lived eighteen years longer than the little sister I had once hoped would disappear from her crib during the night, stolen by an evil fairy, or dead at the hand of a careless *Fräulein*.

At sixty-five I must have been resigned to aging and death: I can remember no raging against the night, no anger about what Yeats described as 'decrepit age that has been tied to me/As to a dog's tail.'

But seventy. This is different. The month at seventy seems disastrous, so without redeeming moments that, in despair, I am taking notes, hoping to find in the recording process a positive value to living so long, some glory to survival, even vainglory if true glory is impossible.

These are my notes, edited here and there to insert the right word when I could find it, to correct the syntax or grammar, and to reduce the excessive rhetoric, the bloated use of the first-person pronoun, that always accompanies one's private record.

July

*I*n the *New York Times* I read a memorial notice placed there
by the publishers of Robert Ferro, a novelist and my friend who
has died of AIDS. Our age has become a time of plague. In
October my editor and friend William Whitehead died of AIDS.
In June I wrote some paragraphs to be read at the memorial
service of an acquaintance, Michael Grumley, a writer and the
lover of Bob Ferro, afflicted by the same inexorable disease.
On that occasion, I quoted from Thomas Mann's *The Magic
Mountain:* 'The only religious way to think of death is as part
and parcel of life.' Now I find that lofty sentiment unacceptable.
It may be the 'religious way,' but like so much in religion, it is
fanciful and delusive. Death denies life, erases it violently,
leaving only the barest memory of the dead, and that often
unrelated to the living truth.

In my too-easy, prose-slinging way, I went on to quote an
old American Indian saying: 'There is no death. Only a change
of worlds.' That strikes me now as presumptuous and dubious if
one is in doubt about the existence of the next world, as I am
today. I believe now in the void, into which Bill Whitehead

and Michael Grumley and Robert Ferro descended. Yes, and
John Ricksecker fifty years ago. I stand on its edge, suffering the
usual guilt of the survivor. My advanced age is a mortal insult
to their premature deaths.

William Wordsworth:

> The good die first,
> And they whose hearts are dry as summer dust
> Burn to the socket.

Today my heart is dry, and it burns for the good Bill and
Michael and Robert who have died first. And John, whom I
remember more clearly than any other member of the class of
1939. Perhaps I was wrong to think that only the barest
memory survives death.

∽

I note how much less I now read, how much slower, how much
better. My old boast—and it was foolishly true—was that I read
a book a day, since the age of about six. That is more than
twenty-five thousand books in my lifetime, a doubtful
accomplishment, since many of them I have entirely forgotten
and others I remember imperfectly. Did they leave some
imperceptible trace on the edges of my cerebrum, to form the
detritus that provides me with what I call, arrogantly, 'ideas'?
Or did they simply fill up the time I was afraid to spend alone,
as though I might sink into nothingness, the adolescent void, if I
were without a book?

It is hard work to read more slowly. Interest propels me,
curiosity spurs me on, and the idiot desire to finish and get on to
the next book. But when I slow down, I interlard the writers'
words with my own. I think about what they are saying, I
consider their methods, I hesitate before their choices, I
dillydally in their views instead of racing through their styles

and subject matter. Reading in the new way now, I learn.
Before, I seemed to be instructing the book with my superior
opinions.

I write more slowly, having learned from my laggard
reading to relish pauses and interstices. An adaptation of
Schumacher's aphorism: Slow is better. Fewer is beautiful.

∽

Today's mail brings requests from two young writers, both
students in workshops of some years ago. Will I write blurbs for
their forthcoming novels? My first impulse is to say: 'No, you
Young Turk. Why should you be publishing a first novel at
twenty-five or -seven or -nine or whatever presumptuous and
cavalier age you are?' I feel an ignoble rush of envy, having
started so late myself: fifty-three, when one rightly expects an
ebbing of the tide, a diminution of creative energies.

But I say yes, I will read the galleys and see if I can honestly
write blurbs. Guilt supplants envy. I know I will feel pleasure at
reading a good book by students I knew as apprentice writers
and even an ignoble desire to be part of the success that might
come, with luck, to them. I want to help if I can, I realize, as I
stack the galleys on the pile of manuscripts to be read first. A
hand up is worthier than one's own fist grasping a higher rung
of the ladder.

∽

A catalogue arrives in the same mail. COMFORTABLY YOURS it
is titled. I read it with dismay. I must be on a mailing list of
persons old enough to be looking for specially constructed toilet
seats, bars and chairs for the shower, bedding equipment that
raises the legs, lowers the back, vibrates against elderly bones.
YOURS, it says, for *my* comfort. I shake with resentment and

then store the catalogue away safely, for the approaching time when, inevitably, I will need help rising from the toilet.

∽

Where are my keys? I look in many places, some unlikely. Then I try my newly devised approach to losing things. I sit down and march myself through the morning, step by step, recreating my progress from taking in the *Times* at six (and having to unlock doors), to breakfast, dressing. At one moment I am in trouble, uncertain whether I have reviewed every step I took three hours ago. Aha. I go back again and stop at hanging up my bathrobe, with pockets . . . where the keys may well be, since I wore it to get the paper. There they are. They are found, *I* am found, in possession of my possessions, not because I looked everywhere, but because I thought about it. A double triumph over aging's forgetfulness.

∽

What can I anticipate in this day? Nothing. I'd be surprised if anything of interest happens. Therein lies the difference between youth, which is everlastingly expectant, and old age, which has almost given up on expectation.

∽

My friend Sybil suggests she stop while she is out to get a videocassette for the evening, perhaps the film of Isak Dinesen's *Out Of Africa.* She loves to go to movies, while I have not really enjoyed them since Greta Garbo, George Arliss, and Paul Muni retired. I dislike the trouble one must go to get to them: the drive, the parking, the line at the box office, the search for a seat (or two together), the two-hour strain to see over or to the side of a tall man with an Afro haircut or a lady with a bubble coiffure, the smell of popcorn, the sound of ice in Cokes, the audible conversations behind my seat, the too-loud sound system.

So I say okay, let's see a movie at home tonight, recognizing the truth of her reminder that all the things I dislike are obviated by our possession of a V C R. I drink coffee and wonder why I still feel unsatisfied by the prospect. I know why: I prefer books. If we watch *Out Of Africa,* the actress with all the quirks peculiar to her style of acting (Meryl Streep with her mouth-twisting) will replace young Baroness Karen Blixen in my mind, in the way that snapshots of places one has visited obtrude upon one's memory of the place. I resent being saddled with my vision of Gregory Peck as Ahab, Greer Garson as Elizabeth Bennet. I want back my own *Moby-Dick,* my own experience of *Pride and Prejudice.* But I fear they are gone, and the film version—a stronger, more lasting impression than words make?—is what I am left with.

ᔕ

The movie planned for last night was not on the shelf. We watched instead a foolish 'action' movie, a clone of every other one ever made. Every violent or terrifying movie we see hardens me, so the next one requires more blood and terror. Last night I was saved from the substitution for a book that I feared, only to be left with a new mental clutter I must scuttle somehow.

Writing of this dislike encourages me to list, while I sit at my desk waiting for something more useful to arrive on the page, other things I now actively dislike.

• Photography. The whole impoverishing act of 'taking' pictures of family, friends, events, places. Like the actor who replaces the character, the photograph replaces what might otherwise have lingered in memory. For some persons, I believe, scenes go directly from the lens to the film without ever entering their minds.

Perhaps the picture helps one to remember the places one has visited, but ultimately one remembers the *picture* of the place, not the place itself.

• Most new books. They are marred by ugly type made still uglier by sloppy offset printing. Characterless acidic paper. Cheap bindings, three-quarters paper over boards, narrow, unstable cloth binding strips that crease permanently at the spine, fade, do not hold the stamping. Tasteless dust jackets, sleazy, shiny, intended to catch the eye but which instead repel mine.

It may be the fifty thousand books a year printed in unsightly housing, a Niagara of paperbound books, not so much published as produced, that make me recall the books I loved when I was young, with lovely, gold-stamped pictorial cloth covers. Now I find pleasure in fine-press books, handmade, issued in small printings that I can only rarely afford. But when I can: what satisfaction they provide for my senses.

Once, I wanted every book I heard about. Now, I desire very few that are sent to me. Too much is being published too quickly, too much that is shoddy, in the end of too little value.

• Change of seasons. I don't understand how this distaste developed. Once my joy was in seasonal variety, the great moment when leaves began to change, the first snow, the early shift from frozen ground to moist melting, the first day the sun colored my skin. Now, I hate the end of spring for fear of the destructive summer heat, and the end of fall because I have no liking for the cold and treacherous ice. Is it change I resist? Or evidences of the passage of time? Or the threats some seasons pose: falling, burning, freezing?

• People. When I was young I liked everyone I met. Newness obscured their faults and true selves. I was too dense to see beneath the interesting surface. Over the years, I learned. Now, I like very few people I meet, almost none, suspecting their exteriors and disliking what I surmise, perhaps wrongly, about their interiors.

• Speed. I moved fast on a flat, empty plain when I was younger, noticing little of what I was scudding through, remembering less. Now that I have grown stiff and shaky on my pins (as the expression goes), I move slowly, uphill in an arduous climb or thickly through impenetrable woods. I notice everything I pass through with such effort, remember more of the terrain. I am jealous of the effort and the time it takes, true, and resent the old speed I have lost, because my slower pace gives my age away.

My loathing for speed extends to fast cars, planes, rapid talkers, swift up and down escalators, athletes, the computer's cursor, the publisher of instant books, the producer of 'new and improved' products seemingly days after the original was marketed.

I am surprised to see that it is easier to list what I dislike than to conjure up the things I still admire. While there is still time, I will have to work at a more positive vision.

ᔕ

I need new batteries for my hearing aids. They are tiny things, little curls the size of infant snails. Last year I was made to face my loss of hearing, which had clearly begun to annoy Sybil, my dear friend and housemate of many years, and others to whom I turned an almost deaf ear—indeed, ears. But the compelling force to acquire two disturbing, overmagnifying instruments was my realization that the music I heard so clearly in my head (and could remember well although I could not sing it) was not what I was actually hearing, hard as I tried to listen more intently to records and tapes, the radio and television.

When I was young I made sure I heard everything, listened in on every conversation, as though widening my sphere of sound would permit me entry into the larger world. 'I have heard that . . .' was a customary start to my sentences, and 'Have you heard that . . . ?' another. I relied heavily on what I heard in order to fill my conversation and the page.

Losing a good part of my hearing reduced my avidity. Now, I am grateful for hearing less, being left alone with my own silences, away from the raucous world of unnecessary talk, loud machines, the shrill chatter of cicadas in our American elm tree, the unending peeps of baby sparrows who nest under the air conditioner outside the bedroom window, the terrified nightmare screams of the neighbor's child through our wall at three o'clock in the morning.

I acquired hearing aids for use in public places—speeches in large auditoriums, classes, workshops, restaurants, theaters, concerts, other such places. But I find I wear them less and less, preferring not to listen to the conclusions of most speeches, the sounds of dishes at a distant waiter's station, and the confidences exchanged at a nearby table. At some plays it is a comfortable kind of literary criticism to turn the little buttons off so I hear less of the inane dialogue being exchanged by unbelievable characters in a dull and unconvincing situation.

∾

Today is what we used to call, in my youth, the Glorious Fourth. Sybil and I celebrate by reading on the deck in the bright sun, and then straightening up the perpetually untidy garden bed at the front of the house. City gardens are full of dog defecation, candy wrappers, greasy McDonald's sacks, tree droppings.

We pack a supper, join my daughter, who has worked earlier in the day to earn overtime at her newspaper, and walk to the Capitol grounds. Hundreds of couples and families are there before us, but we make a space for ourselves by spreading a blanket, and prepare to listen to the National Symphony play patriotic music, sounds I never do hear because the system is not properly placed to bring them to us. No matter. It is Tony Bennett singing, I am told. When it is time for Placido Domingo, snob that I am, I put in my hearing aids. But still the confusion and talk around us overcome my effort to hear the tenor.

Behind us, young picnickers who can hear as little as I begin to sing 'God Bless America.' Delighted with the sounds of their own voices, they sing the same song again and again and again. They stand up and sway, substituting their loud, tuneless voices for the symphony and the famed tenor, feeling both justified, I suppose, and patriotic.

Then there is a fine, reverberating, garish display of fireworks, weaving upward, spiraling down, and splashing out against the navy-blue Washington sky and the white monument. As she watches wide-eyed and admiring, Sybil tells me that when she dies she wishes her ashes to be placed in one of these bright, showy explosives. Her friends and relatives are to be invited to the display and instructed to stand, their heads tilted back to watch her ashes ascend. When a thousand sparks in roseate form light up the sky, and the consequent oohs and aahs rise all over the Mall, she thinks perhaps she will hear them and feel satisfied with her death.

∽

Tired today. My neck is sore from looking up, my spirit weary from the public displays of loving one's country, not with action but with sentimental songs and flags stuck into the grass before someone's cooler filled with beer.

∽

This morning, working on a novella about my life in Far
Rockaway before I was six, I am amazed by the unbidden
arrival to my pen of a game we used to play with acorns in the
ample plots of soil beneath the elms on Larch Street. Sudden as
lightning I remember the street, the tree, the game. How can
this be? I am no longer the child I was, born with a perfect
photographic memory, who floated through school on its
strength with little or no reliance on reason or thought, or
the adult who was graduated from college Phi Beta Kappa
without having resorted very often to the connective tissue of
logic.

Did it come to me from my mother? I believe so. She was
able to replay every bridge hand of the afternoon from memory
at the dinner table. After fifty, my seemingly infallible gift
began to fail. It took longer to retrieve what once had come
instantly to mind or tongue or pen. Now, my memory is much
diminished, like a hard disk that suddenly fails to deliver what
has been stored there.

I operate with a floppy intelligence, such as it is. The
connections I make are hard-won, sudden flashes from the past,
lucky effluvia from the ripe, aging compost heap that is my
mind. So I remember that street, sun-filled and broad, its curious
name (as far as I know there were no larch trees in Far
Rockaway), and the game my sister and I contrived out of the
hulls and slippery green bodies of acorns.

I feel grateful for the arrival of small pieces of information,
now that the lifelong storage system of my personal computer is
often down.

∽

Six calls today, all from writers. A friend in San Francisco, another at the Writers Workshop in Iowa, one playing hooky from morning work at Yaddo and desperate to talk, one to tell me a publisher has paid fifty thousand dollars for five chapters and a synopsis of his new novel, and two, married to each other but calling individually, each no longer able to stand the ego of the other. They are separating.

Until I was in my fifties I knew only one writer, a fellow journalist named William Kennedy who thought, like me, that someday he would be writing novels. No others. Now the only people I know seem to be writers. I argue about this with myself, wondering if it is not a bad, narcissistic state of affairs. Writing may be a vice peculiar to the outcasts of society, and writers a class of eccentric persons who cling together for support against the outside, 'normal' world.

I wish Mr. Brown, the refrigerator man, would call to say he will install the thermostat. There are puddles of excess water on the floor, and a low, throbbing sound that issues from it. I hear very little else in the house, but I can hear the old machine's dying gasps and watery gurgles.

∽

Late this afternoon I call Richard Lucas, who is *not* a writer, but an old friend, a successful sales manager for a publisher of scholarly books in California. Last year he went on a glorious trip to China for his company. He loved the country and the people but returned with some sort of Oriental bug, he said, that he could not shake. Two months later, the strange virus was still in possession of him because his immune system had gone awry, and he knew, he told me, why he was still so sick. No one else knew. I was not to say.

This spring I saw him at a university press meeting in Cambridge, and his handsome face and body were changed into an old man's visage and frame. He was unstable on his feet, he suffered from a variety of what he called, with a smile, 'opportunistic' afflictions. He was cheerful, and hopeful, and very clearly sick.

Now, on the telephone, he tells me he spends his spare time listening to all of the *Ring des Nibelungen* on CDs. He wonders if it is time for him to stop work. Is there a chance I might come to the West Coast for a visit? I say I will try, having no great hopes but eager to see him again, as well as other young friends who have settled in San Francisco. All of them have an apostolic approach to that beautiful place. Everyone, they think, should come out and live there, and look out at the Bay from the hills and wander Golden Gate Park and eat every kind of foreign food in the Castro section.

It is too late, I believe, for me to live in a new place, although it is not entirely new to me. Once, during the war years, I lived there, on Van Ness Avenue as I recall, and later across the Bay in Oakland when you could still take a cool, foggy ferryboat ride to that city-suburb. . . . I tell Richard to come here to Washington when he is in the East (his company has an office in New York City, like most publishers who went west), but it is a foolish thing to say, to make him believe he will be able to visit me. He says he will try.

After he hangs up, I realize I say this more and more. Not 'I will see you there' but 'Come here to see me.' Age. Loss of the enjoyment of leaving home. I should add that to my list of dislikes I made the other day:

• Travel.

∽

A legal-minded adviser on the radio tells a questioner: 'Get it in writing.' Meaning, I suppose, don't trust the oral agreement or the hearty handshake. Get it in writing. I recognize it is the unspoken command that hovers over the head of every writer every morning, every hour of every day. Stop talking about it, planning to do it, considering the alternatives. Get it in writing.

∽

Growing old means abandoning the established rituals of one's life, not hardening into them as some people think. There are the occasional reunions with people from the past, 'old' friends. Leftovers from places where one once lived, neighbors, office mates from the places one worked or taught. Christmas cards are ritual cords that bind us ('my children are now all out of the nest,' they write on the blank side of the card, 'as yours must be') or the call out of the blue, like the one this afternoon. 'Remember me from St. Joseph's parish in Des Moines? We met at the rectory.'

Thirty-five years ago. My perfect memory fails me. I do not remember, neither the name nor the face nor the occasion. We have not maintained the ritual of greeting cards, and so I have entirely forgotten this man. There were no artificial reasons for getting together, like reunions. But now he is in Washington, and eager to remind me of what I have forgotten.

Should I ask him to dinner, as he seems to hope? No, the rituals have given way. I beg off, being overly committed, or leaving town, or something. I don't remember what I said. I'm sorry. Are your children out of the nest? Of course. It's been a long time. I'm sorry. Goodbye.

I cannot remember his name after I hang up. So it goes.

∽

It is the hottest summer in this city's history. This morning, on the deck where I drink coffee and read the newspaper while looking out at the dry elm and the roofs already wet with humidity, it is already eighty-five degrees at six. I think with longing of the sea, where I was in early June, on the bay end of Delaware, close to the ocean but not yet at it. On that coast there is curiously odorless ocean, unlike the heavily weighted-with-salt smells, the fishy, spicy odors, of Maine.

I chose to spend two weeks there because my sense of being alive depends on periodic exposure to the sea. I need to swim and float in it. I need to sit at its edge and watch its moody, heavy, unpredictable vastness. I must stroll its wrack to find treasures of stone, shell, bits of glass and wood, even, occasionally, a piece of 'sea' porcelain which I fantasize as breakfast crockery from a shipwrecked schooner. The ocean restores to me an acceptance of the way the world is now, consoles me for my losses of faith, optimism, physical pleasure, great expectations, mother, sister, grandmother, and young, plague-ridden friends.

Sunk down into the intense heat and humidity of this July morning, I manage to 'cool off' by thinking of the dunes at Lewes where I sat, shielded against the wind, on a deserted beach. I watched the Cape May ferry make its haughty, aristocratic way across the water, a white wedding cake of a ship on an empty ocean, looking as out of place as a skyscraper would at the beach. My memory restores the ship, the cool sand, the grey eternal sea. Perspiration and mortality sit less heavily upon me.

A remnant of cool air from the night clings to the deck. I finish my coffee and take up my battered clipboard, a piece of equipment as necessary to me as radar to a flight traffic officer. I bought this board in 1960. It has held in its rusty iron jaws at the top of a spotted brown length of board every piece of white lined paper on which I have written to this time. The corners of the pressed board have rounded with use and are now flaking away. In ink, with small script, I have written the names of nine books composed on its surface, their dates, and the places to which the board traveled with me.

Having nothing better to do, the immortal prose I summoned this morning somehow not having arrived, I study the places. Albany, New York. Moody Beach, Maine. MacDowell Colony in Peterborough, New Hampshire. Yaddo in Saratoga Springs, New York. The Iowa Writers Workshop. St. Maarten. St. John, Virgin Islands. A bank of the Delaware River. Cozumel, Mexico. Kailuum, Mexico. Surry, Maine. Lewes, Delaware. . . .

Superstition has persuaded me that the words I require often come not from my hand, my pen, or my head but from my clipboard's thin pressed-board interior. To bolster this belief, I once took a strip of printed plastic left behind by the previous writer-occupant of my office in Iowa, Lynne Sharon Schwartz, and pasted it at the top of the board. It reads: 'In the beginning was the word.'

The day grows hotter. Seven-thirty now. The white page clipped to the board is still virgin, unmarked by me but wrinkled with damp. The only certainty is the firm, commanding way the clip holds the paper, surer of its function than I am of mine. Where is the word according to St. John, with which to begin?

ᔕ

The maid comes this morning. When I was a girl, the last time I had a maid until I came to Washington, my mother called all servants 'treasures.' Why? I wonder. Because she felt she had found them, exclusively? Because they were hers alone? Because they were, theoretically, faithful, of great value to household order, asking nothing but small pay and the rewarding sense of having served well? I think she believed all this of her treasures.

My treasure, a young girl from Puerto Rico, comes an hour and a half late. Still, she is a rarity in Washington because she does arrive. She commands hefty pay, close to twelve dollars an hour if she stays only the few hours she seems to be here. She is sketchy about her dusting. Underneath the beds she never cares to explore, nor behind or beneath any stationary furniture. She is hostile to interior windowsills, seeming to believe they are not part of the house, and resentful of fingerprints wherever they may appear. She leaves bottles and bottle caps, oily rags, and pieces of the vacuum in strategic places so I will know she has been there and used them.

But she *is* my treasure. She does what I no longer want to do, she brings some order and shine to our possessions, she makes the house smell of cleaning agents (even if it is not very clean) and Guardsman furniture polish. In my lifetime I have had too little practice with servants. I shy away from giving her instructions or even complaining about her omissions. I hide in my study, feeling guilty about having her do what I should be doing myself. My mother was very good at the mistress-servant relationship. She believed that the mistress had the upper hand over the treasure. In her time that was probably true. But not now. I am humbly, undemandingly grateful for any action my treasure deems it proper to take.

I cower behind my PC, and wait to go over from the carriage house to the main house until I see the lights are turned off. She has gone. I can have a guiltless lunch, repossess the house, recover from my feelings of inadequacy and failure, breathe in the deceptive odor of Murphy's Soap.

⌒

The mail has come. There are nine brown cardboard book boxes that the mailman, in his customary snit at the volume of my mail, has dumped down in a messy pile in the vestibule. The

letters he sticks through the slot in the door. While I wait for
my usual Progresso minestrone soup to heat up (I am an
obsessive eater who likes repetition in foods, perhaps because I
am too unskilled to think up variations), I shuffle through the
mail.

The usual assortment. Requests for contributions, including
one from a local public television station which seems to eat up
its meager budget with frequent mailings asking for
contributions. A case of the cat consuming its own tail. Three
solicitations of my support for the local opera, the local
Kennedy Center patrons' group, the local Arena theater. An olio
of catalogues including—yes, I knew it was about time for it
again—one from Comfortably Yours.

The clothes in most of the catalogues, sent unbidden, are for
persons two sizes smaller and thirty years younger than I. There
are catalogues for men's equipment, including one for hunting
clothes and one entirely devoted to guns and knives, although I
have not lived with a man for seventeen years. One is filled with
elaborate toys and clothes for children: my youngest child is
now thirty-seven years old.

I am too exasperated to look through the rest. I carry the
third-class mail, the catalogues, the publishers' advance notices,
the requests for money and subscriptions, to the kitchen and put
them into a plastic sack together with the book containers
which, opened, seem to have swelled to twice their original size.
Tomorrow I will carry the lumpy, swollen sack down the back
steps, across the garden, into the carriage house and place it in a
can, to be put outside the garage on the proper pickup days.

To what end this useless, expensive effort for the publishers,
and then for me? I have to dispose of matter I did not send for,
do not want, and resent because it tires me to dispose of it.

David Macauley wrote and illustrated a wonderful book
called *Motel of the Mysteries,* a spoof on the Tutankhamen

discoveries. It supposes that our North American civilization, due to a reduction in third-and fourth-class postal rates, is suddenly buried and destroyed under the weight of *pollutum literatum.* Massive amounts of paper harden into rock, and our civilization is lost to human history for a thousand years.

Carrying the discarded mail from front door to kitchen to garden to pails in the garage, to the alley, I can believe this will happen here. We will all soon be similarly buried and petrified under our junk mail. It will take the discovery of 'a series of writings attributed to the late-twentieth-century Franco-Italian traveler Guido Michelin' (to quote Macauley) to explain how it all happened. Lovely book.

∽

A bad night. I thought of Bill Whitehead and Robert Ferro dead and gone. I wondered how death had seemed to them at the moment of its arrival. I dreamed about the pains of dying. Does it hurt? I seemed to be asking my mother, as if I were a child again and she would know about such things.

When I woke at four, I remembered a poem I once could recite: 'Thanatopsis.' William Cullen Bryant's idea was that death was pleasant, like a dreamless sleep, of which, upon awakening, one says: 'It was my best night's sleep.' At five I was still awake, having decided that the poem eliminated one consoling certainty. Only if one was sure one would wake after the deep, unbroken sleep would one lie down fearlessly. Just so for death.

With that, I was afraid to go back to sleep, got up and made coffee and waited in the living room until I heard the *Times* bounce up on our iron steps.

∽

I meet my neighbor across the alley while I am putting out the
garbage. He is in his bathrobe and has lost a lot of weight. I
don't know his name after almost four years of proximity, and
my ignorance has gone on so long it is too late to ask him. We
refer to him as Mr. Lone Star, the name of the restaurant he
once owned, a topless lunch establishment by day, a gay bar at
night. We assume he is gay; under my workroom window on
weekends young men, their radios turned up to loud, hard rock,
wash their cars, or his boat, or his van. On occasion in the
spring, he drives a motorcycle that he revs up and then roars out
of his garage.

Although once on familiar terms, despite my ignorance of
his name—he no doubt is ignorant of ours—we now say little
to each other. It is an aborted acquaintance which never
developed because none of us made an effort. Now, I eye his
shrunken waistline and diminished stomach, and wonder: Can he
be sick? And then I reproach myself: Not everyone who loses
weight is sick, although at times, in my despair, it appears to be
so. My association with Bill and Robert and Michael, and now
Richard, makes me suspect the terrible affliction in everyone I
see who looks thinner. Like evil: Because we know it to be
within us, we then think it must inhabit everyone else.

∽

This afternoon is my time to tape for the radio. The job I have
had for a number of years is a strange one for me, a print
devotee. Out of a month's reading, I choose four books I have
liked, and write a short review for each, to be broadcast on
National Public Radio on the morning news program.

To write these reviews is an exercise in brevity, even painful
compression. I have somewhat less than three minutes to
introduce a book, describe it to some extent, and provide some
judgments about it. No more than five hundred words. Given

the meagerness of time, I have decided to review only books I like, not to waste precious airtime on diatribes against poor books.

I go uptown to M Street to tape, four reviews at a time. I sit in a silent booth, the engineer on the other side of a glass partition, my producer, Don Lee, in the booth with me because I am not very good at fluent reading anymore. I pop my *p*'s, a mistake that sounds like an explosion on the air. I often read the wrong word, stammer (an affliction left over, on occasion, from childhood), or mispronounce a proper noun. These failures require retaping, of a sentence usually. But when you hear me early on *Morning Edition,* you would never know about these slips. Lee has a device that splices out errors and substitutes the corrected forms. I sound fluent and correct, although he has not been able to do much about the increasing slowness with which I speak.

When I hear myself on radio I think how wonderful it would be if all the failings of growing old could be so easily corrected by technology.

∽

Today my reviews are pretty eclectic. One, *My First Summer in the Sierra* by John Muir, is a large handmade volume, a $785 beauty which the Yolla Bolly Press in California has published in an edition of 155 copies. Elegant paper, endpapers designed and made by hand in Mexico by Otomi Indians, binding handsewn, covered in a handwoven rough linen fabric. Every detail of the production of this book is fine. But the cost is high. My intention is to explain why owning such a book is an aesthetic as well as intellectual pleasure.

The second is *Cavalry Maiden* by Nadezha Durova, a Russian woman who managed to join the cavalry and fight bravely against Napoleon. Stirred by patriotism, a dislike of domestic limitations on women, and a passion for horses, Durova served in the army for nine years, even after her sex was discovered. A curious yet engrossing book to choose, published by a university press, Indiana, that takes chances on such works, to my delight.

A biography of Charlotte Mews. I picked it because I did not know who Charlotte Mews was, and wondered why a novelist as skilled as Penelope Fitzgerald wanted to write about so obscure a figure (to me). Turns out it is a superior biography about a fascinating and talented, if now forgotten, poet. I like reviewing books like this, to educate myself, and then my listeners.

The fourth: a novel by Alice Hoffman, called *At Risk*. Oh dear God, I thought, when I read the galleys on the train coming back from New York months ago, can I bear to read about an eleven-year-old girl who contracts AIDS from a blood transfusion? Every page hurt to read. But it seemed a good book to review. The moral, unspoken but clear, is the vulnerability of everyone to the terrible scourge, and the inhumanity of those who wish to avoid contact with it, or think they can. The victim is a child gymnast, a fine athlete, which makes the story even more poignant.

At noon, I will go into the recording studio, wait for the sign to start, give a voice level, and then, in my stumbling way, read the alembic remains of all this reading, like the kitchen midden of a vanished civilization, into a microphone.

∽

Another hot day. The temperature threatens to go as high as 104 degrees by afternoon. On the deck I find a dead cicada who did not survive the night's oppression, a beautiful creature even in death, with lacy, iridescent wings and a thick multicolored body. Its bulging eyes are far apart and look like offset stones. I take it to my study to save, a reminder of the summer's humid destruction.

For some reason it makes me think of the hundreds of dead horseshoe crabs at Lewes last month, for whom the overly warm water probably proved lethal. They lay in ragged rows just beyond the water line, like dead soldiers, on their backs, their eight legs pulled up and folded inside their huge carapaces as if they had died in pain. Perhaps it was not the heat, but an epidemic of some sort. Or a bad storm at sea which washed them onto the shore and flipped them over, halting any balanced progress back out to sea. Their huge, dark-brown, foot-square shells cannot be overlooked. Even in death they emit the organic smell of the elephant house at the zoo.

But my dead cicada has no odor and only a short, unprotected body. Furthermore, it seems to have died alone, on the deck, not of an epidemic as human beings are now dying, but of some solitary, private affliction.

I set the dead insect on the top of a speaker for my radio. It now lies next to the dried body of a huge moth, a piece of driftwood gnarled into an odd beauty by the sea, and a small yellow butterfly, its wings folded rigidly in death.

I keep such things. Why? They are rarely perfect, whole specimens and I know little or nothing about their life history or the calamity that brought them to their end. Do I put them on my speaker to remind me of the arid end of things? Of our human curiosity about endings? The cruelty of existence that ends in rigidity? As *Time* magazine in its old, curiously inverted style might have written: knows God.

∽

Heraclitus: 'All is flux.'

∽

Another section of the manuscript of *The Habit* comes back to me in this morning's mail. The pain of rejection is heavy and dispiriting. This time the editor, the same one who did such a masterful job of line-editing *Chamber Music,* writes that the book seems 'more willed than felt.' Meaning, I take it, that I *needed* to write this story without being able to convey the emotion it should contain. Or perhaps, that I had not felt it first, or that it had no emotion to start with. I don't know what to think. When one's work is rejected one would prefer to believe the editor is wrongheaded, or blind, or prejudiced, or just plain stupid. But I know none of these are true of Faith Sale, who published my favorite among my novels, *The Missing Person,* although at the time hardly a soul alive seemed to agree with her estimate, and mine, of the book.

Willed, not felt? Who can say? Most of us write because we think we have something of pressing importance to say. Conviction comes first, and then the struggle to find the words that bring it to life on the page. In that sense, every fiction is willed. But the feeling, what Henry James called the 'intensity' of its projection, ah! there's the rub.

I keep wondering if I ought to begin again. There seems to be a ready market for first works of fiction, but sixth? Perhaps it is that the voice is worn out, or has become accustomed and thus unexciting. William Kennedy said bitterly, when he accepted the National Book Critics Circle award for *Ironweed,* that fourth novels are hard to publish—he had thirteen rejections for his.

The first-heard voice can make an editor, then the reader, listen carefully, excitedly, for the new tone, the original cadences. I should choose a pseudonym, ALIGNA PARAGRAPH or FLOPPY F. DISK, and submit the novel under it. I rather incline toward Floppy Disk. Biography for the jacket: 'She is a graduate of Centralia Grade School in Berne,

New York, where her family are pig farmers. Her brother sells scrap metal accumulated on their back forty. Her sister married Petunio String, the harmonica player, and lives in Maine. She is interested in needlepoint work, learning to be a better typist, painting by the numbers, canning, and trying her hand at a second novel, if this one sells.'

Noel Coward: 'We must try not to be bitter.'

∽

The telephone rings. It is one of my daughters. I have not heard from her in some time but still, our conversation is light and without recriminations. You are fine? I am fine. Your lover is well? Good. How is your dog? Still has colitis? Poor thing. We talk in this cool vein for a while as though warmth could not make its way over a WATS line. We finish our exchange, she no doubt convinced she has, for now and some time to come, reestablished, via telecommunication, the necessary bond with a parent. And I wonder: How often would children call if they had no access to company or WATS lines?

∽

I read the food page of an old issue of the *New York Times* I find in the garage—day before yesterday's paper—and come upon a new word: argol. It is a crude tartar, the reporter says, deposited in wine against age. I consider this property of argol and wonder what would happen if it were ingested directly into my blood. Would it slow the inexorable aging process? Then I realize that the hope for a fountain of youth never quite dies in the old, even if the deterrent that offers itself is a crude tartar.

∽

At breakfast this morning, a few days before we will make our trek to Maine to celebrate (the word is not exact) my seventieth birthday in a place we love and with people of whom we are fond, Sybil confesses she is an obsessive counter. She keeps strict track of the number of round slices she gets from a carrot, of how many beans she strings for supper. I realize I now do the same thing. I never climb a flight of stairs without counting the steps. I keep track of the steps it requires to walk to the post office, to the Eastern Market, to the photocopying center. Idiotically, every time I climb my own front stairs I count them. Seventeen. Unvaryingly.

Why do we do this? Is counting a way of occupying time? Of lending importance to the unsignificant act we are performing? Whatever the reason, it is an entirely useless occupation, because I never remember the result. Did it take 320 steps or 340 to reach the market from home? As many times as I have counted, and noted the result, the total is gone from my head when I begin the same journey again. Clearly I do not store the results but draw a certain obscure satisfaction from achieving them.

Since seventeen, when I first climbed the partly restored Temple of the Dwarf at Chichén Itzá in the Yucatán, I have always noted the steps I go up. Then, I imagined myself a priest, ascending the eerie grey temple to perform some grisly sacrifice in the presence of the uplifted faces of a worshipful populace. To be 'on top' was an achievement, a triumph over the faint-hearted friend watching me 'from the bottom.' Perhaps it is of no importance whatever to record here that the number of steps leading to the temple atop the Mayan building is 365.

∽

My early-morning start, at six, usually proceeds in the same way: coffee, the *Times* crossword puzzle. Puzzles are another addiction I acquired late in life. I think I understand why. A crossword gets the pen moving, and since I write by hand, the flow of ink into small white squares sometimes encourages, even facilitates, a further flow of words when I get to my magic clipboard.

There is a certain pleasure in filling in the squares with neat, block letters. I am careful not to touch the lines, not to obscure the numbers. Deepest satisfaction, of course, comes from knowing enough to leave no blanks, and, best of all, to require no scratch-outs or overwrites of my inked-in guesses. Therein lies a kind of purity.

Today, the puzzle's key is the names of the planets in their order from the sun. I have waited fifty years, I realize as I fill them in with ease, to make use of my memorization of that list in college: Mercury, Venus, Earth, Mars, Jupiter, Saturn, Uranus, Neptune, Pluto. All this time it has been taking up space on the hard disk that is my brain. But today I see its single purpose. To do the *Times* crossword puzzle rapidly, this morning.

᠀

After I finish speaking on the telephone to a writer friend, who is now well on in years, I find myself thinking about the importance public notice holds for many people. For some writers (Walter Pincus of the *Washington Post* once said this to me) the appearance of their byline next morning is the daily reassurance they must have to keep their self-esteem high in the world of journalism. A sportswriter told my daughter, who once worked for the sports page of a newspaper: 'I need to have stories in all the time. I'm afraid I'll be forgotten.'

For my friend, lectures, readings, and public appearances are essential. They are his link to the world, they remind him (and he needs to be reminded) that he is admired, even adored, by his readers, that he is a valuable person and a respected writer, a conviction in which, I suspect, he is not otherwise secure. His

travels to colleges, bookstores, public auditoriums, have been a
necessary part of his life, so important to him that now that he is
ailing and unable to travel, he is desolate.

Fame: why is it so addictive to the writer? I read a biography
a few years ago which posed the question: What became of
Ernest Hemingway in his later years? The tragic reply was the
title of the book: Fame became of him.

I wonder: What does fame do to the writer seemingly
fortunate enough to be burdened with it? Does the work itself
come to mean less in itself, and recognition more—everything,
in fact? With acclaim established, is the work then affected? Or
could it be that fame, like money, is an impetus that stirs the
writer to greater and better efforts?

I know well that the need for recognition is addictive.
Oxford University Press sent me recently a brilliant study of the
subject called *The Frenzy of Renown* by Leo Braudy. It begins
with Alexander the Great, 'the first famous person.' Braudy
examines ambition and the desire for fame throughout history.
Rome was a society entirely motivated by the urge for fame.
His section on Jesus is subtitled 'The publicity of inner worth,'
the section on Augustine 'Christianity and the fame of the
Spirit.' The chapter on Dante's fascination with reputation is
superb.

Braudy continues through history, to the arrival of the book
'as a prime new place of fame:' Dante, John Milton, Benjamin
Franklin, Jean Jacques Rousseau, James Boswell (who desired
fame through Samuel Johnson), Lord Byron, Napoleon, Thomas
Chatterton, John Keats. He explores the twentieth century, the
century of the press-agented performer, photography, and the
seductive, democratic possibility of fame for everyone.

Here and there are sentences I have marked: 'Many seek fame
because they believe it confers a reality that they lack.
Unfortunately, when they become famous themselves, they

usually discover that their sense of unreality has only increased.'

And: 'Success needs more success to validate itself, and nothing can finally salve the feeling of incompleteness.'

And: ' "The urge for fame," one recent aspirant has said, is "the dirty secret." '

An extraordinarily interesting book.

∽

I've noticed this in my writer friend: No amount of recognition is ever enough. William James said: 'The deepest principle in human nature is the craving to be appreciated,' which surely is the step before needing to be famous, *known*. Many writers need more, and then more. Praise requires constant renewal and expansion. I knew a young novelist whose first book was very well received. His second appeared to no notice whatever. He stopped work on his third, convinced it would be another failure, began to drink heavily, and ended his perturbed life driving his car against a stone wall. An accident, it was called. I often wonder.

On my shelf somewhere is John Leggett's biography of two such writers, Ross Lockridge and Tom Heggen, who became famous for their first books, *Raintree County* and *Mister Roberts,* tried to write their second, failed. Both were suicides. Both found success so heady that they could not face the prospect of not succeeding in the same way. Despair and death became of them.

∽

Tonight I relax by rereading Anne Tyler's *Morgan's Passing,* my favorite among her books, for some reason. No one asked me to read it, no one is paying me to reread it. I am enjoying it immensely.

For so long, because reading has become for me a kind of

forced labor, I am required to have an opinion about
everything. I never open a book without a pencil and pad at
hand, to record what I think as I go along. Now, more and
more, I am determined no longer to read in that way, but to
reread, slowly. To have a usable, publishable opinion no longer
matters to me. Enjoyment was my impetus in learning to read,
sixty-seven years ago, in the first place. I expect now to return
to that simple spur.

Another resolution: to leave unfinished any book I do not
like. During a long reading life, my rigid puritan instincts have
not permitted such an indulgence. Compulsively, I finish
everything, thinking, I suppose, that a book is like what
parsnips, beets, and oatmeal were in my childhood: I was not
allowed to leave the table until I had eaten them.

When I add up all the literary resolutions of this
septuagenarian month—to read more slowly, to reread the
books I have loved or at least remember having loved (I will
not finish them if it turns out I have been mistaken), and to
abandon all books not worth my time as soon as I know their
lack of value—I realize I am coming into a new age of
self-indulgence.

So: I put aside the galleys of Tyler's new book, *Breathing
Lessons,* which have just arrived and decide, under my new
dispensation, to reread *Celestial Navigation* and others of her
excellent earlier books. I'll let the new one ripen, even age a bit
on my shelf, before I come to it.

$\backsim$

We start our trip north to celebrate my despised birthday in the
cool, green quiet of Maine. Overnight we stay with the
Munsons, Sybil's longtime friends, who have lived in a
rambling, comfortable farmhouse outside of Albany for many
years. Barbara is English, a handsome, heavyset woman with an

easy, constant smile and an abiding love of horses, dogs, cats, flowers, food, children, antiques, the Episcopal Church, and her husband. Paul is from an aristocratic Albany family; he is tall, lean, and equally loving. His talk has a fine, humorous edge to it that modulates his wife's warm sentimentality.

They've lived a life of almost no money, making do, as we used to say of such conditions. He taught English in high school for years, but gave up that activity as 'hopeless.' Now he 'substitutes' on occasion. The Munsons raised and educated a daughter, now married and practicing as a nurse, and a charming, lanky son who is a television photographer, lives at home, and has a girl he hopes to marry, the daughter of a nearby farmer. The Munsons' house rings with lovely jokes and lighthearted reminiscences of the time when Sybil, her husband, and their children lived near them in the city.

I feel somewhat out of it. Still, there is enough lingering warmth and hospitality to go around. We eat well in their little screened-in gazebo on the lawn, and watch young Paul and his girl rescue rabbits that have escaped their hutch. I drink too much and go to bed feeling blessed to be among such people, within the circle of their undemanding acceptance and goodness. I feel, somehow, larger and better than when I left Washington. The prospect of the day after tomorrow is not so terrible.

∽

In bed, I think about surroundings. Now that I am old, they seem to have suddenly become of greater importance to me, although I cannot explain why this should be so. Quiet, for example. What one sees, like the sun going down over the Helderbergs tonight, and the head of the old horse eyeing us from the Munsons' barn.

When I was young I was hardly aware of where I was. Now I remember far too little of those places. I was immune to San

Francisco, Des Moines, Millwood in Putnam County, New
York, Clinton Heights in Rensselaer County near Albany, New
Baltimore, south of Albany, and Albany itself. Odd, isn't it,
how that once-grimy, undistinguished city was a source of great
creative interest and ultimate reward to Bill Kennedy. But not
to me. I found nothing there I wanted to record. He found
everything and used its landscape and population to feed his
imagination and American literature for years to come.

Why was I so oblivious? I can ascribe it only to one thing:
self-absorption. Too many years of my life, I now know, were
spent in the arid deserts of my inner self. Like an adolescent, I
rarely looked out and about me. Now I do, all the time, having
exhausted the unnourishing interiors, and discover to my dismay
there is hardly enough time left to take in everything out there.

∽

Waiting for breakfast this morning, and then in the car as we
drove across New York State toward the Vermont hills to pay a
call on a friend bedded down with crushed vertebrae as a result
of osteoporosis (will much of the rest of my life be spent
visiting the sick of my generation? A preferable alternative to
being sick myself, I suppose), I read some pages in David
Roberts's life of Jean Stafford. A rather mean-spirited
biography, I thought, full of little revelations about her
weaknesses (and of course she had many of the more picturesque
ones, enough to satisfy the avid reader) but unconcerned, in the
main, with the accomplishments of her fine books and stories. A
case of imbalance, in which the biographer undervalues her
work because of the colorful and tragic life she led.

I met Stafford once, at the Payne-Whitney Clinic, when she
was being treated for alcoholism and shared a suite with my
sister, who had had a serious nervous collapse. I remember her as
gentle and shaky, with an already ravaged face and sad eyes

although she was young. I remember feeling afraid of her, as I was of my sister, wondering when they would break out with symptoms of their illnesses. We walked to the Metropolitan Museum and I recall that they took each other's hand crossing streets.

In the biography, Stafford is quoted as complaining to her agent that her children's book was not being 'pushed' by her publisher. The verb stopped me. I had a sudden vision of well-dressed publicity people, their hands outstretched, palms flat against a large book, all their weight applied to 'pushing' the book.

I know such action is necessary in our time, in an overcrowded publishing world of too many books and too few buyers and readers. But pushing a book strikes me as indecorous and unmannerly. Let the book make its own way, even through the thick forest of competitors, compelling readers by the force of its words and its vision. If it needs much pushing it may not be worth anything. If it is pushed hard, its weaknesses may be revealed to more readers than might ordinarily come upon them. Disappointment sets in; the reader decides to stop buying new books for a while. Disaster all around.

The pushers occupy a large part of the New York publishing world. I have gone to parties hoping to encounter some writing friends, only to be swallowed up in a sea of very young, chattering, elegant publicity people who talked only to each other and made me feel as though I represented a dispensable, better-left-unnoticed part of their world. Of course, in this respect, my evident age may be the cause; publishing has many young pushers to whom elderly writers, I suspect, are useless baggage, no longer 'on the cutting edge' of publishing. What a vicious, almost lethal phrase that is.

∽

My old friend Barbara Probst, now in her middle seventies and living near the farm which houses the bookstore she built and ran for many years, now suffers from serious osteoporosis. We stop on our way to Maine to see her. She is wry but cheerful, and determined to conquer her affliction. In the process of turning over in bed, she broke her spine in two places. What infinitely fragile creatures we elderly are. Falls, turns, failures of sight and hearing and mental acuity, we deteriorate almost without noticing it. Or, if we notice, we are filled with unreasonable optimism. Always before we have recovered, come back to normal. Why should it be different now?

∽

We drive on, across a final strip of New York State into Vermont and then New Hampshire, past Peterborough, the town where, years ago, I stayed at an artists' colony to write my first book of serious fiction. Places have a way of inspiring writers, even when they are there to write another book entirely. I recall that Thornton Wilder, a guest there, wrote *Our Town* at MacDowell Colony and used Peterborough for Grover's Corners. In my studio there twelve years ago, I read a dedicatory plaque over the fireplace, thought about it for days, made fiction of its suggestive contents, and then wrote *Chamber Music*. I owe Peterborough much, I think as we drive along its outskirts, MacDowell Colony even more, and most of all, Baetz Studio, where the idea for a novel was born.

And then, much further on, when we cross the river into Maine, where the air smells of salt and fish, I think how much of my sense of the value of peace and inner serenity I owe to my love for Maine. The color of the air turns from New Hampshire green to the grey of Maine. I feel I am home.

∽

At May Sarton's secluded house in York on the Maine coast, I look out once again at the rocks, coast, and sea at the bottom of her long pasture. I think of the July, ten years ago, when I worked there on *Chamber Music*. We visit her for lunch, bringing the crabmeat we all love, and wine. She is in good spirits although she says her health is poor. The medication she takes for heart fibrillation makes her sick. It is hard for her to work and yet, 'I have a new novel,' she tells us. A new puppy, irascible and tiny, occupies old Tamas's space. There is a new cat to take Bramble's place. May has transferred her love from the revered dead animals to the new lively ones, although she says it hasn't been easy.

Indomitable about her physical ailments, forthright in her opinions, she leads the lunch conversation about the natural world, her beloved birds, and people, those who visit her, as well as those who oppress her with letters and demands. She has written herself into a corner where, proclaiming her love of solitude, she attracts isolatos who want some part of her time. . . .

But now that she is ill and age is overtaking her, she understandably wishes she did not live alone. Her neighbors, she feels, do not pay much attention to her.

We leave and start up the coast, thinking of May and her unresolvable predicament: to be old and ill and alone, sometimes frightened, a writer who has written her widely read journals, which express a preference for being alone. She craves critical recognition; the applause of her fans does not seem to be enough.

∽

At last we come to the house in East Blue Hill on Morgan Bay that leads to the sea. We have rented it for the terrible Twelfth.

∽

So. It has arrived, July 12, 1989, the day I find hard to believe in. I have now lived for seventy summers, the season beloved to me for warmth, water, clotheslessness, sun, sand, clear skies. Yet I have forgotten many of those years. I was unaware for too long of much of the time—more than twenty-five thousand days—through which I have moved. Now, I am aware of every moment of every day, especially of the summer days. Now that it is growing late.

The house we have rented for a few weeks is a rambling place, built by the sculptor Lenore Straus, who died recently. Her friend Peggy Danielson, to whom she left it, is here, living in rooms at one end. We have the luxury of the larger set of rooms, which were built by haphazard addition, a process not unlike budding or binary fission. They seem to have grown out of each other. At the same time, the house has the feeling of organic, calculated design as though the interior unity of a devotedly led creative life united the disparate sections.

I establish a routine that, on purpose, will limit my time and space. I consider where I will write in the mornings. As usual it turns out to be in a place outdoors, in the sun, within sight of water, Morgan Bay. The porch is three by five feet, so small that no one can walk in front of me or behind me when I sit there with my clipboard and coffee.

Today I 'turn' seventy. A strange verb, suggesting to me what happens to wine when it becomes vinegar. Will I turn in some way other than years? The day is sunny, the water beyond the porch sparkles. A small sailboat is anchored offshore, from this distance looking diminished, like a child's toy. I remember watching a boy sail just such a boat on the pond for toy boats in Central Park. He pushed it out with a hefty shove, then fell in after it, and had to be pulled out by his nurse, who then spanked him. He cried, not from the punishment, I thought, but because

he had dropped the string to the boat when he fell. The boat
sailed away into the middle of the pond.

∾

I am so immersed in thoughts of aging that I waste the morning.
Sybil comes back from shopping with vegetables for lunch. I
smile when I see beets, recalling the short-lived utopian colony
Fruitlands, founded by Bronson Alcott in New England. A
cardinal rule there was that the colonists were forbidden all
'devilish' root vegetables because they grew downward into the
soil, while leafy vegetables were acceptable. They 'aspired.'

When I cannot write, I think about the pleasures of small
spaces like this porch. If I have to stay in a large place I
immediately reduce it. I do not want a choice of aspects but the
limitation of one, so my mind will stay fixed on what I am
doing and nothing irrelevant will be suggested to me, no
distraction by variety. In one day, I settle into a routine to
match the small space. There are whole areas of any new place
that I will never explore, certainly never stay in for very long. I
have no curiosity about unvisited or unused space, feeling
grateful for the protection of the narrow corner I have created.

As a child, when we went to a summer house in Far
Rockaway, I had to sit in every chair at least once, open every
closet, pee in every bathroom, see the view from every window,
before I felt I could settle down for a while and stay. I was
adventurous and loved the new and unexplored.

In my teens I remember tramping through the thick woods
behind the girls' camp where I was first a camper and then, later,
a counselor, exulting as I put a foot into a tangle of brush. To a
city child, it seemed a jungle, and I thought: 'It may be that I am
the first human being ever to stand in this place.'

The newness of everything. The uniqueness of myself and

my experience. How sure I was, knowing so little history, of all this. At the end of his life, Ezra Pound observed to a friend: 'Nothing really matters, does it?' Today I understand this. At the end, or close to the end, or closer to the end than the beginning, the value of what we once thought mattered is lost to us. Even survival, once so important, money, food, family, country, accomplishment, recognition, fame, even: Pound was right.

He once said to Allen Ginsberg: 'At seventy I realized that instead of being a lunatic, I was a moron.'

Today I feel empty and unconcerned, but not moronic or even mad. I have never thought I was mad. I doubt Pound believed it of himself. He must have listened to the diagnosis from the authorities at St. Elizabeths, grimaced at the stupid mistakes he had made by talking too much and thoughtlessly, and decided to say almost nothing aloud for the rest of his life.

Because I cannot make one sentence of progress in my ms, even in sight of calm Morgan Bay, surrounded by silence and solitude, I begin a letter to an Albany friend who writes me long, satisfying letters which I repay with apologetically short notes. I make a mess of the first page, reread what I have written, and see why. These days, my approach to prose is full of ambiguous multiple choices. I write in layers:

thickly   feeds
richly planted with low seaside-like bushes. I believe the bay leads

                    an impression of
into the ocean. I have a sense of   the sea without its wildness.

    suggest to you
I tell you . . .

                    olio/mixture
This morning my head is a hodgepodge. . . . I know too many synonyms.

No, that's not it. I am too aware of possibilities and cannot make up my mind. How will I settle on one? I am no longer able to do that. I shall let David, the recipient of this letter, choose what he thinks is best, giving *him* a sense of (impression of?) power, editorial control, what I seem to have lost now as I write.

I write another letter, to Jim McPherson in Iowa City, feeling, in a low place of pain, my thousand miles of distance from him. So I ask him questions to which I do not expect an answer or at least not one for some time. How can it be, I want to pose to him, that I am so close to the end when, a short time ago, I was just beginning?

Writing to Jim, I suddenly remember what I saw in June on the water off Lewes, the fine Delaware beach. I was sitting in a low beach chair at the edge of the sea. A motorboat passed me. In it were three white men. Behind their boat they pulled a tall black man on water skis, a beautiful, dark stick figure against the grey sky and light-blue water. I can see his towline, I can see his graceful body move in response to instructions from someone standing at the stern of the boat. On the third trip past me, he fell. His black head was all I could see of him, a period on the grey sentence of the sea. The boat slowed, maneuvered around him, and, in a moment, stopped. Four white arms reached down and pulled him into the boat.

Another man dived into the water to rescue the skis. The thin black man, apparently very strong, lifted the white man and the skis into the boat. Now filled with a satisfying conglomerate of black and white bodies and heads, the skis sticking up from the stern like sawed-off masts, the boat pulled away.

So it may be with Jim McPherson in lily-white Iowa City: the troubled, often frightened, reclusive writer, scarred by his life in the South, sustained by white students and many white

friends, trying to learn to trust and love 'amid the alien corn,'
hoping for safety and protection from hereditary white enemies,
as he saw it, 'out there.'

Once, when VCRs first appeared on the market, Jim used a
little of his MacArthur windfall to buy about a thousand
videocassettes. If his life was threatened, he planned to hole up
in his house and spend his time watching films. He believed the
assault might come in the near future. Once I borrowed a tape,
labeled *A Thousand Cranes.* When I put it on the machine he
had loaned me, it turned out to be *Rambo 2.* How many of them
were in the wrong box? I wondered. How many surprises lay in
store for his future days of seclusion?

∽

The terrible Twelfth goes on. I invite Peggy, our host, to share
May Sarton's gift of champagne with us. Friends from up the
road, Ted Nowick and Bob Taylor, will come too. I suddenly
think: A more suitable way to celebrate this dread event would
be alone, not in society. I ought to let go of the cheerful
illusions of company and surrender to the true state of old age,
remembering Virginia Woolf's conviction that at bottom we
are all alone and lonely.

The sun moves to the other side of the house. I go in to
change to slacks and a shirt with sleeves. In the process I do an
unusual thing. I look skeptically, exploringly, at my body in the
floor-length mirror. In my young years I remember that I
enjoyed feeling the firmness of my arms and legs, neck and
fingers, chin and breasts. Once the result of such examinations
was less reassuring I stopped doing it. Thereafter, I never
resorted to a mirror, believing it would be better not to know
the truth about change and decline. In my memory of my body
nothing had changed.

Now I look, hard. I see the pull of gravity on the soft tissues of my breasts and buttocks. I see the heavy rings that encircle my neck like Ubangi jewelry. I notice bones that seem to have thinned and shrunk. Muscles appear to be watered down. The walls of my abdomen, like Jericho, have softened and now press outward. There is nothing lovely about the sight of me. I have been taught that firm and unlined is beautiful. Shall I try to learn to love what I am left with? I wonder. It would be easier to resolve never again to look into a full-length mirror.

∾

I open mail I have brought with me. A letter asking me to 'read' at a conference on creative writing. My first response to the invitation: pleasure, ego gratification. Someone remembers and wants me still. The second: a quick reminder. I dislike reading my work aloud, hearing all the errors that are, too late, cemented into print, noticing the rhetorical slips, the grating infelicities. The sound of my own voice gives a terrible legitimacy to faulty prose. I say no. But thank you for thinking to invite me.

Another letter asks if I am willing to be nominated to the Senate of Phi Beta Kappa. Out of the blue. I have had no connection with the society since I was elected to it fifty years ago. At that time I had to explain to my father, one of this country's nastiest anti-intellectuals, what PBK was. He laughed, and directed my mother to attend the induction ceremonies, adding that he was far too busy to come out of his haberdashery store on the Bowery to go to 'Phi Beta Krappa.' A long, hearty laugh followed that witticism, in which, as I recall, my mother and I did not join.

I say yes, for the usual reason. I always figure I will not be alive when the time comes to do anything about this, or, as likely, I will not be elected. I never say yes to invitations to speak or read or teach if the proposed time is a month or two

ahead, believing that there might be a chance I will be living
when the time comes. But a year from now is very safe.

I ponder the vast unlikelihood of PBK's selection of me,
after all this time, out of its 300,000 members. Did my name
come up on some computer screen, as the result of random
choice? My acceptance of the nomination is as unlikely as the
coincidence (it seems to me) of its coming upon me. To all this
happenstance, I say an unbelieving yes.

∽

Sallie Bingham, whom I have known since we met at the
National Book Critics Circle's yearly meetings (or perhaps it
was the National Book Award ceremonies in the early
seventies), sends me a copy of *The American Voice,* a magazine
she publishes in Kentucky. There is a small essay of mine in this
issue.

When we first knew each other in New York, I had no idea
who Sallie was—a daughter of Kentucky's most famous family,
as it turned out—until her family sold its interest in the
Louisville Courier-Journal and the story of the family's
internecine war was revealed. I never guessed she was wealthy:
my Sallie Bingham? She was shy, unassuming, quite willing to
lunch at my suggestion at a grubby sandwich shop. I assumed
she was probably in New York on a small budget from the
paper for which she worked as book editor.

Now she uses her money to assist women writers and to
publish the magazine *The American Voice,* in which this short,
sad piece of mine appears. I read it with dismay, wondering how
I could have brought myself to display in print my grief at the
deaths of Bill Whitehead, Lazarus, the fish, and the sight of the
moribund Florida lions.

This is what I wrote on growing old:

Everyone does who survives. The inevitability of it is

offensive to me, but what is to be done? To choose not to is oblivion, and do I want that, yet? No. I prefer half a loaf, a piece of the stale pie, diminishment, a slant of light, to total eclipse. The flowers of my life wilt, they lose their fragrance and their colors, but I cling to them, preferring them to nullity. I hear less, see crookedly, lose weight and height, grow spotted and stolid, placid and inept. A writer named Guy Davenport reminds me that for Edgar Allan Poe time was the unstoppable tread of death. This sound I hear more clearly than once I did, when the steps were muffled by activity and love, or drowned out by my hot pursuit of notice and satisfactions. I used to fly; now I linger or stumble. Once, it was always dawn; now it is twilight.

I collect metaphors for death. Driving down US 1 toward the flat and unexceptional Florida town of New Smyrna Beach, I pull over onto the shoulder of the road. I get out, and walk toward an elongated boxcar with grillwork at the sides. There, in three narrow cages, are six tired, sick-looking lions, with yellow, aged manes and flabby, ineffectual paws. Their eyes are full of tears. Scabs line their mouths. They lie in sawdust and excrement, haunch forced against haunch, and their flesh hangs upon their bones like drapery.

They are stationed there to call attention to a display of secondhand Chevrolets. Their trainer (keeper?), who wears knickers and a jungle shirt, flips his whip in the direction of the parked lines of dingy automobiles. We do not stir, so fascinated are we by the boxed-up captives who look as though they may be dying. He tries to enliven them by poking at their legs with a pointed stick. They do not stir. He flashes his whip across their faces. They stare back at him, understanding perfectly but too weary, too sick, too wise to obey.

Two children standing near me scream with delight at the sight of the six princes of the jungle now reduced to proletarian paupers. Children love animals, I think, even stuffed ones. These prisoners, locked into their coffers, especially delight them. The children are free; these poor guttersnipes are down on their luck, recumbent, enslaved. What a pleasurable turnabout, I imagine they are thinking.

The children move away, toward the cars, holding their parents' hands. I stand still, enclosed like the abject lions in the unreasonable quarters of my old body, confined to the bars and sawdust of a future that can end only in the black light of oblivion. What remains of their lives is a dirty joke, told with a snicker by an obscene keeper in cowboy boots, holding a taunting whip. What remains of mine is not much more elevated: There are too few years left to make another life. My age is my cage; only death can free me.

Or:

My friend, the editor of two of my books, dies. His death is not a solitary phenomenon; many others are dying of the same irrevocable disease. The tragedy of his death, and the death of others, is that they are all young. Their talents have been blasted away by a God seemingly blind to their value and deaf to their prayers and the prayers of their friends. Feeling older than ever, I board a train at seven in the morning, a shining silver bullet aimed at a straight shot up the East Coast from Washington to New York, depended upon by this aging body to get me to the Hotel Chelsea on Twenty-third Street in time to bid my friend goodbye, to tell him how much I will miss him, how I despise the irrational fate that determined it.

Would I have said these things? I will never know. Arrived at the door to his apartment, I find he is not there. His friend, Tony Blum, tells me he died three hours ago. Bill, a man at the height of his physical and intellectual powers. A young man (to me) who understood the value of full friendship with this old writer. I rage against my own survival in the darkness of his disappearance, I hate being an age he will never see, I detest his leaving before I can bid him farewell.

Oddly, I cannot cry. I am too angry with the God I trusted to save him, to lift his affliction. All the way back to Washington tears press against my eyes, but they never come. Two weeks go by. I do the ordinary household things to ready our home for the winter. I sweep leaves and bag them into fat plastic sacks, I store the lawn chairs and drain the hose. I wonder what to do about the pair of black goldfish who live, against all lack of care and expectations, in the small pond in the garden.

I note the temperature. They must be brought into the house before the frost expected this evening. I scoop them up into a wide enamel basin (all I have on hand), fill it with water, and leave them on the deck while I go uptown to buy (at a place called Think Tank) a bowl for their winter housing.

When I go to transfer them to their new abode, one is not there. I cannot believe it. Where can he be? The mystery of this absence overwhelms me. And then, looking down, I see his bloody body on the deck. He has committed suicide, I decide, leaping out of the basin onto the destructive wooden floor. Stuck into the wound on his head is a dead wasp. I put the survivor, whom I now name Lazarus, into the new tank, take the body of the suicide into the garden, and bury it, placing a cross made of matchsticks over the grave.

And then I cry. For half an hour without being able to stop. For the dead, nameless fish, for Lazarus now left alone and lonely, I believe, for my carelessness which allowed the nameless one to die, dashing against the slanted side of a merciless washbasin to his solitary death.

I am amazed at my free-flowing tears (I do not cry easily, perhaps five or six times in my adult life, which now stretches to

half a century), at the depth of my grief, at my obliviousness to
the true cause of my sorrow. Now I know: I am crying for my
dead friend, not alone for the newly dead fish. At last I am able
to flood his memory with my hot, resentful, furious, contrite
tears. I realize I am trying to wash away my guilt at having, at
this late age, survived his youth, my remorse at my health in the
light (darkness?) of his undeserved disease. I place crossed
matchsticks over the memory of my love for him, my vision of
his bright face and endearing young smile. I surrender to the
inevitability of all death and the injustice of his early one. I
mourn my late arrival at his door, my unspoken words of
farewell and love.

I mourn the fish. The moribund Florida lions. The odium of
growing old, the perversity of not growing old: the whole
inexplicable condition of life and the illogic of its termination.

$\backsim$

I read over this record of what I felt. At the time I thought
putting it down on paper would assuage my suffering. Now I
know nothing will do that. I used to believe confession (in the
dark upright box with the sound of the priest breathing on the
other side of curtain) would take away my sins and guilt. No.
Nothing will, except time, age, forgetfulness. Even then . . .

We drink champagne with Peggy, and Ted and Bob, our
Washington friends who now live most of the year in East Blue
Hill, Maine. Someone says something about seventy being
young these days. I smile and say nothing, thinking of
three-year-old Emily Galvin's birthday party in Iowa City. Her
mother, poet Jorie Graham, read to her after the feasting. When
Jorie went to answer the telephone, I asked Emily if she wanted
me to finish reading the book to her. 'Oh no,' she said,
withdrawing in horror: 'You're too old!'

~

Sybil and I have a quiet dinner together at a restaurant in Blue
Hill overlooking a small stream and waterfall. We talk about
everything but this day. I am grateful for her tact. I don't know
how much more celebration I can bear. We have wine, but no
toasts. I think how wise she is not to propose one.

All day I have been doing what we do each end-of-year
period in the bookstore: I 'take stock,' a curious phrase. For
books it means counting what we have on the shelves. For me,
today, it meant looking at what I had and have and was and am
and did and do, what I no longer wish to be and do and keep
and acquire. I try to find some sound philosophical basis for
what I have been, and fail. All I can conjure up is bits and pieces,
nothing solid, nothing whole. My lifelong, hard-held views:
where are they now in this reexamination? What do I believe?
What have I done? The time I have been granted: what has it all
come to?

I look across the table at my friend, who is happily paying
the bill for our good dinner, as a final gift for the terrible
Twelfth, and wonder, under the confusions of the day and my
amazement at having survived this long without being aware
that all this time had passed: Who am I? At the end of this hard,
dismaying, and only occasionally heartening day, Sybil and I
talk of someone we have heard about who, it was reported to us,
died, 'leaving nothing.' The phrase stopped me. Its ambiguity is
interesting. Does it mean money, property, goods, books,
'belongings,' as they say? In a different sense, perhaps it is more
accurate to say we die leaving *everything:* what is left of the
beauty of the natural world, the familiar faces of those we have
loved, the music we have come to know so well that it plays in
our ears without the use of technology, the paintings engraved

on our eyes, the interior vision of dancers who perform
brilliantly in our heads while we sit inert in our chairs at home.
All this we 'leave.' It is never nothing. It is everything.

ᔕ

As I fall asleep, I remember that I have not spoken to Richard
Lucas in many days. I feel the need to be close to him now, to
be part of his suffering and his courage, to *see* his dying. Am I
being honest, or is this feeling accentuated by the impossibility
of gratifying it? We are three thousand miles apart.

This desire is something new for me. When I was a child I
would not look at the dead, would not accompany my mother
into a hospital to see a sick friend (in those days children could
visit their friends without hindrance). 'I'm afraid,' I remember
saying. 'Of what?' she would ask. I could not tell her, I did not
know.

During most of my life I walked away from the sight of an
accident, sickness, suffering, as if, by my not witnessing them,
they would cease to exist. Forced, by chance, to look upon an
old man who had been shot through the head in front of his
cigar store at the corner near my apartment house in New York,
I am unable to forget the sight, in my dreams, and awake: a
piece of the shell of his skull was left on the sidewalk after the
ambulance had taken him away. As a young girl, all of death,
dying, suffering, and pain coalesced into that glimpse of a
section of a dead old man's head.

I could not bear to look upon anyone who was less than
perfect for a long time.

My grandmother took great pleasure in the spectacle of
death. She used to attend funerals regularly, most often for
persons she did not know. The Frank Campbell Funeral Home
was three blocks from where she lived. As I recall, she had no
particular sympathy for the living, except for her close relatives,

whom she loved devotedly. But she was proud of her own
survival to a great age—ninety-three. The longer she lived the
more she seemed to enjoy funeral ceremonies for strangers.

Clearly she was comforted by the number of deaths she had
survived. I can still see her, dressed in her decorous black caracul
coat, her black fur cloche set firmly on her white head, a
matching muff over one gloved hand, in the other hand the
Union Prayer Book, walking slowly from the Hotel Milburn,
where she lived for many years, towards Amsterdam Avenue.

Once I walked with her as far as the door to Campbell's. We
stood among the mourners, waiting for a plain pine coffin to be
carried into the building.

'It must be an Orthodox Jew,' she said. Of most of the rites
of her faith she was ignorant; she refused to attend Temple
Rodelph Sholom, which her mother had helped to found,
because it had begun the practice of charging a hefty fee for the
use of the pews. But from her constant funeral-going, she knew,
and much admired, the frugal Orthodox practice of using a pine
box instead of an expensive 'casket.'

She added with evident pleasure, 'It will be a long and very
sad event. A lot of crying. All in Hebrew, the prayers I mean of
course.'

She went in. I went home.

⟳

The day after. I have survived the twelfth. It is a clear and
lovely early morning. I am, kindly, left alone on the deck. In
my nightclothes I sit here and watch the light grow stronger. I
too grow stronger as I drink coffee and consider this new day.
The day after. I have survived *that* day, I have made the turn.

I begin to read galleys of a novel I brought with me, *The
Swimming Pool Library* by Alan Hollinghurst. It is an account of
gay life in Britain in the sixties, when sexual activities were free,

joyous, unshadowed by the specter of fatal disease. The characters are cultivated young upper-class men who speak affectionately about well-known homosexuals and go to baths seeking constant stimulation with young boys, handsome blacks, other beautiful young men of their own class.

Hollinghurst describes their unending sexual adventures most graphically, in pickup motion-picture theaters, in salons of great private houses, at pools and body-building spas. The narrator, William Beckwith, is the grandson of a judge-aristocrat, Lord Denis Beckwith, for whom he has great affection. At a bath, William saves the life of aged Lord Nantwich, and thus becomes involved in his life and the proposed editing of his diary.

His grandfather tells William about being at the first performance of Benjamin Britten's opera *Billy Budd,* and hearing E. M. Forster criticize some of the music, especially Claggart's monologue:

'He wanted it to be much more . . . open, and sexy, as Willy puts it. I think *soggy* was the word he used to describe Britten's music for it.'

Years later, the young narrator, his lover, James, and Lord Beckwith see the original tenor of the opera at a performance: 'Pears was shuffling very slowly along the aisle toward the front of the stalls, supported by a man on either side. Most of the bland audience showed no recognition of who he was, though occasionally someone would stare, or look away hurriedly from the singer's stroke-slackened but beautiful white-crested head. . . . James and I were mesmerized, and seeing him in the flesh I felt the whole occasion subtly transform, and the opera whose ambiguity we had carped at take on a kind of heroic or historic character under the witness of one of its creators. Even though I felt he would be enjoying it, I believed in its poignancy for him, seeing other singers performing it on the same stage in the same sets as he had done decades before, under the direction of the man he loved.'

Hollinghurst manages to suggest in this passage a parallel between Pears and Britten, Captain Vere and Billy Budd. This performance of the opera, 'an episode in his [Pears's] past,' is somewhat like the elderly captain's memory of the blessing of Billy Budd. But I may be reading this into it; Hollinghurst may not have intended the suggestion. More than this, the portrait of sick and aging Pears being almost carried to his seat by aides is as poignant for the reader as the opera must have been for the tenor.

The old, gay lord's diary contains a moving portrait of dying Ronald Firbank: 'I had noticed a solitary figure sitting across the room, also drinking freely, even heavily. He was slender & beautifully dressed, of indeterminate age but clearly older than he wanted to be. He must in fact have been about 40, but his flushed appearance & what might well have been a discreet *maquillage* gave him an air of artifice & sadly made one feel that he must be older, not younger. He was not only by himself but in some heightened, almost dramatic way, alone. He squirmed & twitched as if a thousand eyes were upon him, & then composed himself into a kind of harlequin melancholy, holding out his long ivory hands & admiring his polished nails. His gaze wd wander off & fix on some working-boy or freak until an appalling rasping cough, which seemed too vehement to come from within so frail & flower-like a body, convulsed him, doubling him up into a hacking, flailing caricature. After these attacks he sat back exhausted & quelled the tears in the corners of his eyes with the back of his trembling hands.'

I suppose these tender, intense portraits of the sick and the aging through the eyes of young men (the young lord goes with his friends to join Firbank for the evening) strike my sympathies now as they might not have twenty years ago. I read on, further than I intended this morning, compelled by the force of these portraits.

Absorbed by the poignancy of these scenes, I suddenly remember sitting in the orchestra of the new Metropolitan Opera House (it will always be the new one to me), watching the aged Maria Jeritza being brought to her front-row seat by two stalwart, handsome young men. She leaned heavily on their arms; but her majestic head in its customary white fur hat was held erect. Her face was so heavily powdered it was almost unlined, 'whited out,' it seemed. She wore dark sunglasses, her body was small and soft. She seemed ageless and frail. The young men deposited her carefully in her seat, the patrons around her applauded. She bowed her head from side to side in gentle acknowledgment of the recognition she seemed grateful for.

From time to time I looked her way during the performance of *Der Rosenkavalier*. She never moved her head, she seemed to be absorbed in listening. I could not see her eyes behind the dark glasses.

'Doesn't Jeritza look wonderful?' I asked the man in the seat next to me during intermission. 'She always does,' he said. 'That floppy hat, that wonderful face. You'd never know she was blind.'

∽

Radio up here is a movable and most uncertain feast. After an hour of National Public Radio, a music commentator with a delivery even slower than mine takes over. He occupies long minutes with his tortoiselike news report, so plodding that I cannot bear to hear him out. A nuclear explosion could have taken place somewhere. At the rate his announcements are made, I would never listen long enough to learn of it.

Turning off his news in the middle makes me feel unaccountably free. No news is good news, the old saw goes. On the air, on TV, in the newpapers, good news is an oxymoron, an impossibility, since so little good is happening, and what there is does not make for interesting 'segments.'

In our time, 'news' means tragedy: car accidents, rapes, murders, robberies, train and airplane wrecks, deaths from cancer, heart attacks, and AIDS, criminal acts in the high places of government, academe, the Church, highly-placed-family feuds, and lost, stolen, or battered children. Mistreated wives. The homeless and mad who freeze on the streets. The unemployed and desperate lower middle class. The hungry poor. Wrongly discharged mental patients. Drug addicts, dealers in coke, heroin, crack, and smack: what hard, almost vicious names for the false escapes that the displaced lower and unhinged middle and upper classes indulge in. Corruption. Bigotry. Revenge. Terrorism. Rebellion. Nuclear threats, leaks, breakdown, wastes. The breakdown of the environment: polluted water, air, destroyed forests, reduced ozone layer. The greenhouse effect. All news.

At the same time, when we are told about them, these catastrophes are so common and expected that they pass along the semicircular canals of the ear to the auditory nerve without creating a single tremor in the heart or the mind. It is not that they are bad news, they are hardly news at all. They *are*. We hear and read about them, see them on the screen, and accept them as accompanying, almost unnoticed, the act of being alive in a bad time.

The absence of TV and radio and the ten miles we would need to drive to town for a newspaper are no deprivation. They are a respite, a lull in the customary, numbing avalanche of human misery and despair, the decline, perhaps the imminent destruction, of the race.

∽

We have dinner with our friends up the road. There is kiwi
fruit in the salad. I had always thought kiwi was a long-beaked
bird to be seen in New Zealand, but recently I have learned it is
a fruit with a rough brown skin and tart green interior. Very
fashionable. I have tried it before but cannot develop an
affection for it.

I realize that foods introduced to me in childhood and
adolescence occupy all the available space for acceptance by my
taste buds. Mousses, spaghetti squash, pastas of all sorts,
radicchio, pita bread, and a hundred other new arrivals on
menus: I cannot grow to like them. My enduring passions for
food are tied to ancient memories. When I was five, my nurse
took me to a pork store on Broadway. The butcher offered me a
slice of liverwurst, the casing carefully removed. I still shiver
when I think of how wonderful that taste was; I still try every
kind of liver sausage in a vain attempt to recover the intense
pleasure of the first piece.

I remember the first spear of fresh asparagus, bathed in
butter, that my mother offered me. It has never tasted quite the
same since. If ever I am blessed with a garden I will try to grow
that wonderful vegetable in an attempt to recapture the initial
bliss. Other such irreplaceable memories: the first sweet potato,
creamed spinach from a glass box at the Automat, mashed
turnips and carrots, the soft remains from the broth of a boiled
chicken: carrot, celery, livers and gizzards, parsnips and onions,
one glorious mishmash of flavors, eaten from the strainer with a
wooden spoon. Wonderful.

No kiwi, no papaya or mango, can come close. My tongue
and taste glands are incapable of further education. If there is not
a long, comfortable, worn precedent for the food, it is now too
late. I grew up in an age of somewhat colorless American

cooking; the new interest in foreign and native cooking has
passed by my old-fashioned palate.

～

The last, fine day on the bank of Morgan Bay. I have not grown
weary of looking at the water, doing nothing, thinking idly in a
haphazard sort of way. Thoreau began his book *Cape Cod* (I
have an edition republished by Houghton Mifflin in 1896 with
delicate little watercolors by Amelia Watson that appear in the
margins of the text) by denying this is so. 'When we returned
from the seaside, we sometimes ask ourselves why we did not
spend more time gazing at the sea; but very soon the traveler
does not look at the sea more than at the heavens.' How long
would I have to stay before this indifference set in?

～

Before we leave Maine to go back to the humid, unpleasant
city, I telephone Richard in San Rafael. His voice is thick, as if
his tongue were swollen.

'I have thrush,' he tells me with an effort. I think first of a
small speckled brown songbird, shake my head angrily at the
inappropriate thought (much as I had last night to kiwi), and
say something stupid like 'I see.' Then I remember. In the old
days, children got thrush, white spots in their throats, a fungus, I
think. Richard, my young friend, so hopeful when last I saw
him, is now host to a childhood affliction, together with all his
other adult infections.

～

Washington. I come home to the mail, an avalanche of brown
boxes and envelopes, about fifty review books for the ten days
we have been away. My daughter Elizabeth, who lives around
the corner, has watered the plants, fed the fish, and stacked

books in large piles. The mail fills a post office bin. I think of something I read recently, by Marina Tsvetayeva: 'I am indifferent to books. . . . I sold off all my French ones; whatever I need, I shall write myself.' This would be a good resolution for me.

∽

Sybil has gone off happily to work in the bookstore, relieved, I think, to be back in her familiar milieu of friends dropping in to talk about books, neighbors, customers, other dealers. She is a social soul. I often think she finds the isolation of a long vacation with me and only a few occasional friends very trying.

I, on the other hand, sink back into hours of solitude in the carriage house with great pleasure. Does one enjoy solitude more in old age because it is a preparation for the long loneliness, as Dorothy Day called it in another context, of death? Once settled into my study, I move out of my growingly unresponsive body into my head, where I can reside comfortably for long periods of time. It is an effort to come out. Time passes slowly in that abode, more slowly for me than in the world of events, noise, movement, and people.

The first day back: I cannot settle into writing. I forget to bring the clipboard over from my luggage in the house, so, naturally, I cannot write a word. I decide to stretch out on the hardbacked, hard-cushioned couch and find myself making a list, in lieu of anything better to occupy me. I decide to do it in the form of questions rather than statements of fact, because assertions no longer come easily to me. Questions are a more suitable rhetorical mode.

a] (better, more algebraic and ambiguous, than 1) Is there anything of significance I still wish to acquire?

b] Is there anything I have that I no longer wish to keep?

c] Is it possible, at this late date, to lead a life based on principles, a guiding or ruling philosophy?

d] Do I take as seriously as I should the fact (this one irrefutable) of my mortality?

After all my childhood joys and terrors, and shallow adolescent anguish; the shock of October 24, 1929, when the stock market crashed and my father, 'wiped out' as he said, put his head down on the dining-room table in the middle of dinner and cried, at about the same time that my best friend's father, whose name, I recall, was Robert Dince, took his life by jumping from a window of a tall building in the garment district of New York; and after the exhilaration of learning how to learn and reason in college; after the suicide (or accidental death) of my friend John Ricksecker, who jumped (or fell) from the roof of the School of Commerce on the last day of classes of our senior year, his arm catching on the no-parking stanchion, stopping his fall for a moment, and then coming off at the shoulder; after the war, in which we women served, and were served by the elevating symbol of the uniform we wore and the power of elating and irresponsible love affairs; after the short-lived postwar optimism during which I had children because I believed the world was going to be better, we would be extraordinarily successful and, someday, very rich; after the slow descent into the present, marked by the dissolution of family ties by death and divorce, by the dilatory liberation of blacks and women, by the minute beginnings of a recognition of overt sexual diversity and androgyny (what in my youth was called 'perversity'), by the gradual disappearance of traditional forms of religious belief, of hopes for peace after Korea and Vietnam and Cambodia, of faith that the forests were protected, the rainwater, springs, and water table pure, the cities safe, interesting, and clean; and after my sad loss of patriotic conviction that this is the smartest, most ethical, richest, and most trustworthy country on the face of the earth, of certainty that medical science's injections and pharmaceuticals are a sure protection against most viruses, bacteria, germs, fungi, I have come to this age of anxiety, despair, and hopelessness. All this has happened in my lifetime, in two-thirds of a century. This morning, listing it all as I lie on the couch, I still have no firm answer to the question that continues to plague me:

e] 'Who am I?' Or the question that runs parallel to it: 'What has my life meant?' Somewhere Nigel Dennis wrote that you are your name, no more. With what I had faith in removed, changed, deleted, my name may well be all I have left. Still, it is a first name from my parents, the other part from my husband, not much of my own.

∽

Tonight, after a day spent trying to change the despairing contents of my head, I read back over the last page, and venture to put down some answers.

a] No

b] Yes. Almost everything. There are notable exceptions. My CD player and disks, this PC on which I am now rewriting, the sixteen-volume *OED,* my VCR and collection of sixteen operas and ballets on videocassettes, designed to fill evenings when I am too tired and too old to go to the new Met, the State Theater, the Kennedy Center. Two goose-down pillows and one electric blanket, my clipboard, the Library of America volumes, Sybil, my children, my grandson, a few irreplaceable friends. The order is haphazard.

Nothing else I can think of at this time.

c] I don't know. Perhaps I never was able to.

d] No. I cannot entertain (wrong word?) the thought for

more than ten seconds, at last careful count.

    e] I don't know.

∽

I took today off, went to the pool, swam as long and as hard as I
was able, and then lay in the shade, afraid to indulge my passion
for sun on my spotted and aging skin. 'Off,' I think, what a
strange, ugly, truncated adverb. The day off. At the airport I hear
'I am off to Nova Scotia.' I watch the plane take off. On TV
the commentator says, 'He's off the track on this one.' Off
my feed, my game. On and off. After enough repetition the
little grunt-like word seems to mean everything and then
nothing. Gertrude Stein: 'If anything means anything, this
means something.' I suppose.

August

*D*espite the terrible heat, I have agreed to go to Boston to give a talk. I dislike making speeches, but I hate readings even more, so this is the lesser of two evils. Sybil points out, when the day comes to go and I complain loudly, that I had only to say no at the time I was asked. I explain, once again, that I say yes to invitations issued a year or so in advance because I am quite certain I will not be alive when the time comes. So I am polite and agree to do whatever it is.

I stay at a Marriott hotel where my lodging has been arranged. Chain hotels have grown so large and efficient that they are no longer humane. The door to my room opens with what looks like a credit card. Faucets have levers and buttons, not handles, and I can never figure out whether to push, pull, or turn them, and in which direction. To the right? The left? Up? Down? The buttons on the TV are no longer functional. One must operate it through a cable box. The instructions for this are complicated and located knee-high.

A questionnaire in the shape of a chatty letter from the owner of the chain asks for my views on the equipment and

service. The communication is almost as complex as income tax
forms. Each system in the room, every electrical appliance, is
listed, and I am asked what I think of them all. These polite
inquiries are intended to suggest that the management *cares*
about me. The replies, I suspect, will interest no one.

No longer do I check out at the reception desk where a
friendly, pleasant lass, or lad, bids me goodbye at six in the
morning and tells me to please come again. Not a chance. Now,
sometime after midnight, my totaled account is pushed under
the door. I leave the key on the desk in my room, telephone to
inform a machine I am departing, hoist my luggage on my
shoulder or pull it along on its wheels (no bellboy at that hour).
I creep 'off' into the still-dark morning, feeling like a
impecunious boarder escaping the payment of rent. But I know
my charges will not be ignored as I have been. They will arrive
on the American Express bill three weeks later when I have
forgotten I was ever in Boston.

ᔍ

The extraordinary heat of this summer is attributed to what is
called the greenhouse effect. No one except scientists seems
especially worried about it because it is so cosmic a concept that,
like the thought of death, no one can contemplate it for more
than a few seconds. The world will end in heat and fire, we are
told. In addition the ozone layer that surrounds this planet, an
area I never heard of before this summer, is severely threatened.
Further damage to it will cause skin cancer and glaucoma
among the world's population.

Where are the old, set-in-stone verities about the familiar
earth? Like a rock slide, like an avalanche, they are falling,
wiping out what we thought was our sure footing. Birds in all
their awesome variety have abandoned the seashore. The gulls at
Moody Beach in Maine, where we used to summer, have left

the shore and gone inland to Route 1 to lunch and dine at the
refuse heap behind Howard Johnson's. They dote on the
remainders of fried-clam plates.

∽

Today it is too hot to write on the deck at the back of my long,
thin Victorian house. The fine American elm between the house
and my study is afflicted by what appears to be, in early August,
premature senility. Leaves droop, the trunk seems to hang down
like a dispirited elephant's, instead of lifting up above the
carriage house. The branches are wilting and look too tired to
serve the tree. Squirrels and cats, who usually lead a noisy,
adversarial existence in the backyard, are somewhere else. No
birds are here at all, as if they too are so affected by the wet heat
that their feathers have dragged them down into some cool,
subterranean hideaway.

   Is the elm aging, like me? I notice I am unhealthily aware of
signs of growing old, everywhere. At the Munsons' last month,
I noticed their endearing way of surrounding themselves with
old things: the horse, their aging dogs, the elderly cat with its
deformed ear as the result of a hematoma, trees that they tell us
are close to the end of their lives, antiques for sale in their barn
that look as if they had reached the extreme edge of possible
endurance. I admire their hospitality to less-than-perfect old
animals and, I like to think, people. Like me.

∽

The summer heat has increased the number of homicides in this
city, once a peaceful place. The streets are dirtier than I can ever
remember, more crowded and, I learn from the evening news,
full of people exchanging stolen money and goods for drugs.
Recently, a woman was attacked across the street at one in the
morning. Sybil heard her cry out, 'Help me!' Sybil leaped out of

bed, awakening me (my deafness prevented me from hearing the cry), dialed 911. A few minutes later the police were there, a small group of people had assembled, an ambulance roared up. Next morning we learned the young woman had been knocked down and her shoulder hurt by a young black male who had left a car to push her down and grab her purse. He then ran back to the car and sped off. Across our quiet, 'safe' street.

∽

So the city grows ever more threatening. At night I park my car (which was stolen and trashed last spring by a fourteen-year-old boy) and sit patiently in it until I am sure there is no one on the street. I walk to the market with money in my pocket, nothing else. I feel myself becoming paranoid and what is worse, racist, and I hate the feelings.

I wonder how long I will be able to see some humor in my beleaguered state. The boy who drove around all night in my car until the police caught him had jimmied the ignition in order to start it. A policewoman in Anacostia called to tell me the car had been found. 'Come and get it,' she said, 'and bring a screwdriver.' A screwdriver? 'Yes,' she said. 'To start it. Your keys may not work in the car.'

I hung up. Then I heard myself laughing. I had forgotten to ask if I should bring a Phillips-head screwdriver or the common variety. I decided to take both. The car started with a key, I was relieved to discover. I drove it home with a smashed passenger-seat window, and a huge spiderweb of cracks on the windshield caused, the policewoman told me, by a bullet. No sign of the bullet. 'But I'm glad to say it's not in the boy. Not a bad boy. Just having a joyride.'

Not a bad boy. I suppose not, when you consider the murderers and gang-war packs and drug dealers she has to deal with every day. This boy who breaks into and steals cars is

hardly a criminal deserving of much attention. His thievery is
the fourth such event for us. Wayward Books, our out-of-print
and medium-rare bookstore on Capitol Hill, has been robbed
once, broken into twice. Now it is equipped with bars on the
windows and an alarm system. My car also has an alarm system
which turns on the horn and the lights if it is entered without a
key. Only our persons are without such protective equipment. If
I am mugged or knocked down, as somehow I constantly expect
to be (cowardly as I have grown), I can only resort to the
now-familiar cry: 'Help me.'

༄

Walking though the variegated, interesting streets of Capitol
Hill I come upon three slender trees growing close together,
upright and companionable, swaying and seeming, at the top, to
bow decorously to each other. The little triangle, or triple
alliance, reminds me suddenly, for no reason I can think of, of
the decorative element, said to be representative of bundles of
bamboo, on the beautiful face of the palacio in the ruined,
ancient city of Kabal, in Yucatán.

   It is a mystery to me why I remember Maya at this moment,
and at so many other times since my first sight of the ruins more
than fifty years ago. Stimulated by a view of a
nineteenth-century facade somewhere on my walk to the market
in Washington, the awesome grey stone surface of a building at
Uxmal will come to me, suddenly. I feel the hot breath of the
god Chac-mool as he sits proudly at the top of the Great
Pyramid at Chichén Itzá, and then a kind of spinal shock as I
recall the first sight of the Temple of the Dwarf rising up into
the blue morning air at Uxmal, silent, solemn, not yet invaded
and diminished by hordes of camera-laden and straw-hatted
tourists.

Solitary, majestic, honorably old, the ruins at the once-great cities shame the garrulous little Mayan guides and gatekeepers who stand at their bases. The hallowed ruins defy change and death. They do not age; they seem to have finished aging. I have a memory of myself standing at the top of their great heights, a young girl, looking down arrogantly, triumphantly, in the shadow of the small, rectangular temple that caps the ascent of steps. At seventeen I am totally absorbed in celebrating having conquered the challenge of the almost vertical (or so it seems) staircase.

At the bottom stands my traveling companion, shading her eyes to look up at me. She is Margaret Schlauch, professor of English at New York University, the first woman to be made a full professor with tenure at her college. She is in Mexico to compile a Nahuatl grammar of the Aztec tongue. I am here as an undergraduate student at the Universidad in Mexico City. Twenty years separate us, dramatized by my flashy ascent of the temple, her patient wait at the bottom.

Fifty years later, the January of my sixty-eighth year, I am the aging woman watching Kate, my daughter, make the brave climb, her brown head an echo in sepia of mine half a century ago. I know what she is feeling. In youth I imagined myself a member of the priestly caste, performing sacred rites on the elevated platform for *hoi polloi* at my feet. But in old age, unable to make the climb, I become part of the people, respectful and worshipful at the bottom.

Passage of time is embodied in these ancient stones, one resting immutably upon another. Radiant serpents slither down each side and end in open-mouthed, long-tongued wonder. I wave back to my elevated daughter, envying her youth and energy, resenting my age, awed by the immortality of the temple.

I know a little of medieval France and England, and have
studied ancient Greece and Rome, and the nineteenth century in
the United States. But Maya is the only civilization I have
yearned to be born into. I would like to have lived in the classic
period, the Puuc period, that produced great architecture,
astronomy, mythology, mathematics. In those years men and
women believed that feeding human blood to the soil would
increase its fertility. As a young Mayan, I might have rebelled at
this terrible waste of human life, but perhaps not. Since birth I
would have been part of a deeply believing community,
ignorant of the concept of the sanctity of the individual life,
indeed, unconcerned for my own.

With the great mass of people I would have stood on the
great plains around the pyramids of Palenque, Chichén Itzá,
Uxmal, Kabáh, Sayil, gazing up reverently at the little party of
priests in their robes and feathers, belts, armbands, and masks. I
would wish, as all the others around me must have done, to be
raised in the eyes of the Chac-mool and Kukulkán, even at the
price of what we knew was happening in the warm air hundreds
of feet above us. To be raised to that platform meant instant,
ceremonial death. I see myself, a young virginal girl, rejoicing
that I am chosen, my breast about to be sliced open by a sharp
stone knife, my heart lifted out of my chest cavity by holy
hands and laid in the little bowl embedded in the lap of the
great rain god.

The Chac-mool's stone head is turned away from the sight
of the bloody muscle, his cold eyes royally aloof. He is scornful
of any human price for his favors, expecting it always to be
greater as his attention wanders and he looks away. His
expression suggests: Blood is cheap, a small price to pay for the
gift of water in this arid peninsula. It will take the blood of a
whole population to satisfy my immortal thirst. His knees
drawn up, his back curved, his feet bracing his recumbent body,

the Chac-mool ignores my still throbbing heart. He almost smiles at the insignificance of the offering.

Now when I visit Maya I neither climb nor stand very long watching others go up. I walk across the great plain at Chichén Itzá to where the flat platform of the Skulls sits, with its row upon row of grisly heads, eye sockets with no eyes, unfleshed jutting jawbones, filed, pointed teeth lining the absent mouths. At that time, in the late winter before my approaching birthday, I thought about the Mayans, building, carving, worshiping, exultant in their sacrificial moments of religious fervor. Still, they must have turned their eyes to this grim platform of human remnants as if to remind themselves that the glory at the top of the hundreds of steps, in the hands of painted holy men heightened by feathered headdresses, ends here among the skeletal heads, one very much like the others.

And the Chac-mool sits up there, grinning into eternity, suggesting to me that it is not so terrible to die if you die in a sacred place at holy hands in a rite as pure and holy as rain. Like your Christ, he says, my custom is to accept blood and change it to water to serve the soil and bring forth maize and bananas, coconut and papaya. Death is for the living: It is a very good thing.

Deep in this fantasy, I am still without my heart when Sybil comes back from the bookstore to have lunch on our deck. It turns out to be too hot to eat outdoors, so we retreat to the kitchen and I pull myself away from thoughts of death and bloody sacrifice.

∽

We decide the cure for Washington's terrible humidity is to go to the beach. It is so hot here that one can believe in the world's approaching extinction. Is it possible, I wonder, to live long enough to link my own end with the world's? The thought of

death is always made more terrible because it runs parallel to the
even more unbearable idea that the world will go on without
me.

When I was a child everything in the future, like the past,
seemed to be permanent, immutable. The years, the centuries to
come that I believed I would live, were set, like Mayan cities, in
stone. Now, to my shock, it is clear that nothing may remain.
Not for long. It is even possible I, or my children, or perhaps
my grandson, will be a part of the final earthly solution.

So we drive two hours to the Delaware shore. At the sight
of the ocean, ignoring the bodies on the jammed beach from
which the odor is not of salt but of suntan lotion, I feel restored,
fresh, and almost young.

Water to me is a saving grace. As a child I forgot my anger
at my parents or camp counselors or teachers if I went to a
swimming pool, or to the lake. (At that time I had not learned
about the cleansing and restorative power of the sea.) I would
pull through the water, feeling the power of my arms as I did
the Australian crawl, cupping my fingers to push towards the
bottom, beating against the surface with my toes pointed
ostentatiously, as though a divine Coach was watching me from
above and I was showing off, with every stroke, for the elevated
Spectator.

Water was freedom, an element in which I believed I had
perfect control. Lake and pool waters were calm enough to
provide that illusion. I moved through water in a kind of
ecstasy, cut away from the rules of the land, social requirements,
limitations, disapproval. Water was action, more effective than
prayer. When I swam I believed in God. In later life, the act of
prayer brought me closer to believing in Him.

Water is my best and oldest friend. I trust it. On land,
always my adversary, I have little sense that my body is any
longer a good servant that will obey my orders. My ankles have

weakened; I am always in fear of slipping, stumbling, and being hurt when I fall. This fear is not groundless, to make a poor pun: Twice I have broken ankles, many, many times have I sprained or strained them. My arms will no longer lift my thickened body easily out of chairs, out of the bath. My back hurts under the stress of lifting or bending, or sometimes for no reason at all. I stub my toes, jam fingers, feel the irritations of pollen and dust in my eyes, nose, throat. My teeth are loosely rooted in my gums, which have moved back under them. From the pressures of accumulations of fat, my skin has loosened, leaving my chin and neck, breasts and buttocks, abdomen and thighs unsightly to me. Everywhere my skin is ornamented with wrinkles, brown spots, roughened places. Cups of flesh have appeared beneath my eyes. My once-firm, reliable body, quick to command and as quick to respond, now moves in slow motion, dry to the touch, weary, lax, unresponsive.

But in the water: I return to the state of my youth. I move without fear. There is nothing to collide with. Miraculously, I am upheld by a force greater than my arms and legs could apply. I turn fast, acquire some speed, advance, retreat, rest, and start again without effort. My old friend, water, my good companion, my beloved mother and father: I am its most natural offspring.

September

Somehow I have survived this torrid summer. It is the fifteenth of the month, the birthday of my friend Margaret Schlauch, who died last May before she reached her ninetieth year. For much of our lives we were out of touch. She lived halfway around the world for the last thirty years, but always I felt a strong connection to her. From her publications I knew that she was still intellectually active well into her eighties, writing scholarly papers and books in obscure, disparate, but always valuable fields: Icelandic and Norwegian sagas, Chaucer, Emily Dickinson's style, James Joyce's *Finnegans Wake,* the effects of society on language, other linguistic subjects. I had always assumed, despite the difference in our ages, that she would outlive me, for her life was purer, more peaceful, full of higher aims and purposes, and single, without family or children to distract her.

Maggie and I met in 1936 when I was a seventeen-year-old college student and she, an awe-inspiring professor of English at New York University, was thirty-seven. In those years the coeducational college at Washington Square in New York was

called the downtown campus to distinguish it from the uptown,
all-male branch of the university called the Heights. We met
downtown in the Village.

The course I took with her was in medieval literature. To
this day I remember how impressed I was by the *Nibelungenlied,*
the *Völsung Saga,* the gentle lays of Marie de France, the Norse
Edda and Icelandic sagas, the sad tales of the Tuatha De Danann,
the *Romance of the Rose.* The beauty of Beowulf and the Pearl
Poet persuaded me to study Old English and then Middle
English so I could do graduate work in Chaucer. Maggie's
enthusiasm for the Middle Ages was so great that I began to
think of the twentieth century as a degraded, almost
retrogressive time, a descent from the glories of 1400, the year
of Chaucer's death.

Maggie was a superb teacher. Her homely, likable face
would light up when she talked about the beauties of a language
that, in most cases, I could approach only through translation.
After a few months of her instruction I was converted by her
scholarship and transferred from the philosophy to the English
department.

At the end of an interminable and boring sophomore year,
Professor Schlauch and I were on good terms. Once she invited
me to a little 'evening gathering,' as she called it, at her
apartment on Christopher Street. There I met the poet Eda Lou
Walton, her friend Ben Belitt, Edwin Berry Burgum, a member
of the English department whose field was the European novel
(I remember he talked about a writer named Kafka of whom I
had never heard), and other impressive persons. They all
appeared to be calm and relaxed in their achievements, far
removed from the world I inhabited of avid, ambitious students.

I heard Professor Schlauch tell the others she was planning to
spend a year in Mexico, compiling a dictionary of Nahuatl, the
language of the Aztecs. Suddenly I wanted to go to Mexico to

study. I was heartily sick of college, except for the courses taught by the brilliant and stimulating Sidney Hook and by Maggie, I was tired of the Village, the arty bohemian bars, the fights in front of the Jumble Shop where we picketed because the restaurant wouldn't admit 'Negro' students, the squalid, long subway ride every morning to Sheridan Square from the Upper West Side and then back again late at night after the Reading Room closed. From the small 'foreign study' office I wangled an exchange fellowship to the Universidad de México and persuaded my parents I was old and wise enough to leave home, school, and country for part of a year. I was free. I gloated.

Early in June, Maggie, her Irish mother, and I sailed to Havana aboard the *Morro Castle,* a year before it sank. There we stayed a month while Maggie learned Spanish quickly (she already knew and spoke about ten languages), and I struggled to acquire a bit of the language. Her mother, as I recall, found it an ugly and incomprehensible tongue and refused to use it.

Fulgencio Batista was in dictatorial charge of the country. I remember being frisked when we entered labor meetings in Havana, the kind of gatherings Maggie liked to attend. I had known of her strong labor sympathies at college; she was a founder of the Teachers' Union and the Marxist publication *Science and Society,* and a faculty supporter of the American Student Union, of which I was an active member. In Cuba and later, during our time in Mexico, she was drawn to workers' gatherings and labor meetings; among my old pictures I have one of us seated in a box at a labor hall where Vincente de Toledano was giving an impassioned speech.

I remember a visit to the seaside village of Batabanó, where the inhabitants fished for sponges. A small, bright-eyed boy offered to show us a wonderful sight, he said. We accompanied him to the Catholic church, the most impressive structure in the village, in a class with the residence of the operator of the

United Fruit Company and the priest's rectory.

Inside the door of the Spanish-style church, the boy reached above his head and pushed a switch. His eyes shone with wonder at the sight. A statue of the Virgin, close to the door, had lit up. Around her head there was a crown of electric light bulbs. Her eyes were two bare bulbs. At her feet another circle of bulbs illuminated the snake on which she stood. In her mouth, in place of teeth, Mary sported two rows of small, white, glowing bulbs.

I gasped. The boy stared at the Virgin. *'Muy buena,'* he said.

Maggie said nothing. Afterwards she used the visit to the church to illustrate her strong antireligious sentiments. The only electricity in the village was here and in the rectory, she pointed out, so the boy's idea of beauty had been malformed by this ugly vision. I had seen it differently. I was moved by the look in his eyes, the devotion with which he looked up at the Virgin's glaring features, the way he genuflected at her feet before he turned off the switch.

It was a memorable, exciting year in Mexico. We studied (well, perhaps it is more accurate to say that *she* worked and studied while I played and flirted with handsome Mexican boys) and, on weekends, traveled, to the great Aztec ruins and to the west coast, where we walked about the sleepy town of Acapulco, swimming in the warm, blue water, and finding a native family who put us up for the week. There were few tourist hotels built then. It was a lovely, quiet village.

Everywhere we traveled I had the sense of discovery. Once we went down the neck of the Yucatán peninsula and up its horn by rickety, life-threatening buses that seemed to hang over the edge of the sheer Sierra Madre cliffs. We stayed in Il Progreso, a seaside town where we hired an ancient taxicab to take us on the six-hour drive to Uxmal.

The Mayan driver stopped his cab at the edge of what looked to us like aboriginal jungles, thick, tangled low growth extending in every direction. He told us he could go no farther. 'No road into,' he said. He would wait right here and pointed into the bushes in the general direction of the ancient city of Uxmal.

Maggie and I walked two miles on a barely discernible footpath, stepping into tangles of vines and extricating our feet with difficulty. We came upon a great carved stone lying across the path. Was it a representation of an animal skull, a mask? A live, antediluvian-looking iguana, grey-green and wise-looking, sat beside it. We exploded with uncontained excitement at our feelings of awe: We were, we thought, the first creatures to come upon these sights, these wonders.

Then I stumbled and looked down to see what had tripped me. My pride at the uniqueness of our exploration faded. There at my foot was an empty green Coca-Cola bottle, probably left behind, I was later to learn, by a Carnegie Institution archaeologist who had been working on the site for ten years with a large team, uncovering the temples and the ball court.

After college, Maggie helped me to obtain a scholarship to Cornell. The long separation of our lives began. Once she visited me in Ithaca, I remember, and I was enormously impressed by my Cornell English professors' respect for her. Then I married, moved about, and the war came. My husband and I both entered the service. Maggie and I continued to correspond, she sent me offprints of her articles, the war ended, and then there was a long silence during which we were out of touch.

In April 1952 I came upon an article in the *New York Times* entitled 'Journey for Margaret.' It reported Maggie's decision to leave the United States for political reasons, and to go to work and live in Poland. Then a letter from her arrived, mailed in Warsaw. She wrote that she had decided she would not take the loyalty oath when, she thought, New York University would demand it of its faculty, because 'I am a dedicated Marxist, no matter how undogmatic.'

Her odyssey was extraordinary. She had dismantled her apartment, given away her books, and settled her aged father into a nursing home. She left Montreal without a passport and flew to Copenhagen. The Polish ambassador took her from the plane and put her on one to Warsaw. There she joined her sister, the wife of Polish physicist Leopold Infeld, who had been in exile during the Hitler years and had returned to head the department of physics at the University of Warsaw. He expedited her establishment at the university, where she originated the department of English studies.

She was to live in Warsaw for the rest of her life. Often she traveled abroad, to Scandinavia, to England, and at least twice to the United States, always using a diplomatic passport. When she was in the United States lecturing, I went to the University of Connecticut at Storrs to see her, and then she gave a class at the College of Saint Rose in Albany, where I taught. Once we met in New York to hear *Fidelio,* at the 'new' Met, a reunion of significance to us because we had heard the opera together thirty years before in the lovely old building on Thirty-ninth Street and Broadway.

It was fine to see that she was the same likable, sharp, modest, affectionate woman she had always been, intellectually ageless and still enthusiastic about her writing, teaching, and research. By now her fluency in Polish and Russian equaled her extraordinary command of the Romance languages. We laughed about the disparity in our linguistic skills. I asked her if she was still able to read Nahuatl. She said she hadn't tried recently. I had to confess I had forgotten most of my Spanish.

I asked her if iron-curtained Poland had lived up to her hopes for it when she emigrated. She said, 'Of course, one is always somewhat critical of some things in any country. It is inevitable. But I have never regretted my decision. I am with my family [by now she had a brilliant young niece and nephew, and her widowed sister Helen had become an accomplished translator], friends, and colleagues, and a wonderful succession of students, eager to learn English and grateful for whatever I am able to teach them.'

I told her I had thought of her and her half-Jewish niece and nephew during the recent anti-Semitic activities in Poland. She was silent for a moment and then she said quietly: 'I was glad that Leopold was dead.'

During the last intermission we walked about the beautiful crimson, crystal, and gold opera house. I wanted to know if she liked the building. She said she thought it was very fine. But how much had our seats in the orchestra cost? At the time I think they were almost twenty dollars apiece. We recalled the old days when we had paid fifty-five cents for each seat in the family circle, looking out at the wonderful, exalted ceiling, the red-lined boxes, the gilt decorations, and the brilliant chandeliers. 'All this beauty,' she said slowly, with, it seemed to me, some reluctance, 'for the very few.'

That was our last meeting. We wrote on occasion. Then her letters stopped. Three of mine went unanswered. My last attempt to contact her was a long letter I wrote from the Villa Serbeloni in Bellagio, Italy. The Polish Minister of Culture visited there for a three-day conference while I was in residence. I asked him if he knew Professor Schlauch. He said of course he knew *of* her. Was she well? He thought so. Would he deliver a letter to her? He hesitated. I said I would leave it unsealed. He said yes, he would try. He would not promise, of course, that he would be able to locate her.

I spent the evening writing. At breakfast I gave him my thin sheets of Rockefeller Institution stationery in an open envelope. I never heard from her, nothing about her from anyone, until the spring of 1987 when my reliable informant (on death matters), the *New York Times,* published a short, laconic obituary. Teacher, scholar, an expatriate who became a Polish citizen after World War II, she had died in a nursing home in Warsaw, survived by her sister, a niece, and a nephew. Nothing more. Nothing about her learned accomplishments, nothing of her successfully communicated enthusiasms for the world's great if little-known literature, so that egocentric, self-satisfied students (as I had been) were brought out of themselves into the dark yet illuminating religious fervor of the Middle Ages.

Had I been the obituary writer I would have added something about her curiously profound understanding of a time so steeped in God that men died and murdered for Him (as the Mayans were doing a hemisphere away), curious because it came from an atheist, a convinced Marxist. In our time the religious spirit that suffused every aspect of human life is long gone. Now we tend to secularize Him, 'to see Him only in our neighbor,' Thomas Merton wrote. Prayer has become horizontal, not transcendent, not 'fiery prayer' as the Fathers of the Egyptian desert practiced it.

Maggie was a fiery scholar, a defender of an age whose profound faith she did not share. But she understood it, because her passion for Communism ('no matter how undogmatic') resembled it. I picture her spending eternity not in a plebeian downtown campus but at some ethereal Heights, teaching with the great prophets and sages. Had she lived until today she would have been eighty-eight. I miss her.

৩

My daughter Elizabeth lives on Sullivan's Island in South Carolina. She sends me a clipping from the local paper about a significant event occurring in Myrtle Beach. A bill is being sponsored by Representative Tom Keegan 'to ban dwarf-tossing' in that state. He thinks the activity 'not only degrading but dehumanizing.'

What is dwarf-tossing? Just what it says. A nightclub audience has been entertained by the spectacle of David Wilson, a midget, being thrown into the air. The newspaper does not say if it was a contest to see who could throw Wilson highest or farthest or hardest or most often. Or whether there were other small persons tossed at the same time. Wilson wore a protective leather harness and a neck brace and landed on air mattresses. Nonetheless, a few days later, he died in Gainesville of what was said to be alcohol poisoning.

This did not end the entertainment. The club held another dwarf-tossing. Informed of the bill before the state legislature to stop 'the fad,' as the manager called it, the manager disagreed with Keegan's view that the contest was dehumanizing. 'Why would a dwarf be doing it if it was?' he demanded of Keegan.

Why, indeed, I wonder. For notice? For money? Because there are not too many employment opportunities for midgets? Because cruelty to defenseless 'freaks' and animals, small children, and women is common in this society. A misdemeanor charge, with a two-hundred-dollar fine for thirty days in jail, will not cure the common human need to be cruel to anyone who is weak, obscure, and small.

∽

Each year at the end of September I spend a morning gathering up my files and correspondence so they can be transferred to the University of Virginia Library, where my 'papers,' as they call them somewhat ostentatiously, reside. Today I find, under the files waiting to be transported, three letters that must have escaped my last donation to the library.

The first is from May Brodbeck, chancellor of the University of Iowa when I taught at the Writers Workshop

there. She wrote to me in Washington from Iowa City
(September 20, 1980):

'I spend the exhausted evenings—when I can—either at
concerts (the Cleveland Orchestra tonight!) or reading: *New
York Jew,* which I loved, of course, an old Sarton, and de
Beauvoir's *All Said and Done.* She's not a nice person, I've
decided, narcissistic and politically too naive for a grown-up
woman. On your recommendation I've just bought Shirley
Hazzard's *The Transit of Venus* and cannot wait to start it. Then
I'll go back to Italian novels, to keep the language up. I've
bought two season tickets for the concert series; perhaps when
you get back here we can share them.'

May Brodbeck was a philosopher of science, pushed up the
demanding administrative ladder because of her calm, steady,
logical way of thinking, and her objective but kindly treatment
of everyone with whom she dealt. After years of enduring 'the
exhausted evenings,' she retired, went to the West Coast, bought
an apartment, and, a few months after settling into it, took her
life.

The other two letters were from Esther Senning, a longtime
friend of my husband's from the years they spent in Ithaca at
Cornell University. Esther lived in a partially restored
farmhouse in Voorheesville, near Albany, when my husband and
I and our children lived close by. We visited the Sennings on
Sundays and watched their four children grow up along with
ours. Her husband, Bill, a New York State official in the
Conservation Department, used to entertain the children by
standing on his head at the age of fifty. One day an aneurysm
burst in his head; he has spent the rest of his life in a nursing
home. Only a small portion of his former physical and mental
capacity survives.

Esther raised and educated her children, visited Bill once or
twice a week, and sometimes, with help, brought him home for

the weekend. She was a gallant, lonely, cheerful woman who
loved cigarettes, music, art, and literature, but the Fates (perhaps
more accurately the Furies) gave her no peace. One of her sons
fell deeply in love, married, had a child, and then was deserted
by his wife. He lived alone near us, in Gaithersburg, and called
once to arrange a date for dinner. Before we could meet, he
climbed on his motorcycle, left his helmet at home, and drove at
full speed into a wall. Esther mourned him quietly. A short time
later she developed cancer of the mouth, refused the operation
that would have disfigured her face, accepted less radical
chemical treatment, and went on living alone with her affliction.

On January 27, 1977, she wrote to me in Washington from
her farmhouse in Voorheesville: 'And now the news. The cancer
is gone or arrested. I can hear again. I've got up off that couch
and am able to take care of myself, even drive. I'm pleased about
the last two, but oddly enough, I'm not so sure how I feel about
being rid of the cancer. It's like having to die twice. I had
accepted it when I declined 'adequate' surgery, figured I'd had
seventy pretty good years and was ready to settle for that. And
the kids had come to terms with it, even to Bert's [her youngest
son] bringing himself to say he'd like to make the pine box for
me, which I said I'd be very proud to be buried in. I felt as
though I were attending my own wake, at least receiving last
rites. And now we all have to go through all this again. I feel
I've conned people into getting more than my share, or at least
crept down and looked at my Christmas presents ahead of time.'

I wrote to tell her that, as literary editor of *The New
Republic,* I often got duplicates of books. What sort of books
did she enjoy these days? In February she wrote: 'I like all of
Faulkner and John D. MacDonald, Kurt Vonnegut, Jr., Adam
Smith. All of Robert O'Neil Bristow and both of Richard
Bradford. Merle Miller's Truman thing, and Jane Howard's *A
Different Woman.* I like John Cheever, Janet Flanner, Kingsley

Amis. Anthony Burgess confuses me, but I'm willing to try him again. I liked *Portnoy,* couldn't stand the bloke who wrote *Myra Breckinridge.* Or Auchincloss.

'I wonder if the common requirement I have for books is learning how different people manage to get from womb to tomb, even from day to day. Because for me it's a real stinker, propelled by momentum and dumb hope, deriving sustenance from a Picasso here and a Beethoven there, or a passing cloud and a few hearty laughs now and then. Why do I go into all of this? I'm really jollier than I sound.'

Less than a year later she was dead.

I put the letters into a correspondence file to send to Charlottesville. I shall probably never see them again. Although I have no photographs, the faces of those two friends are clearly present to me. I never found out who Robert O'Neil Bristow is, or Richard Bradford, for that matter, and I don't know to whom May Brodbeck gave her second set of concert tickets when I did not return to Iowa that year. These mysteries, like the end of Margaret Schlauch's life, bother the novelist in me. But the friend I was is enriched even by my incomplete memories of them.

∽

Sybil calls me from the shop. She sounds close to tears. We have been broken into, there are records, papers, books all over the floor, and our cash is gone. I abandon plans for a morning with the clipboard, throw on yesterday's clothes, and walk over, faster than I usually am able to travel.

This is our second break-in since June, the same month in which my car was stolen by the 'not bad' boy. The first time the robber came through an upstairs, barred window from the roof. This time he broke a front-window pane and squeezed through into the front of the shop. Two months ago, a thief cleaned out

the cash box while Alan Bisbort, our manager, was putting
books away at the back.

Sybil quickly becomes philosophical, after we have cleaned
up, and after the police have come by to hear her story. They
try to sustain her with tales of multitudinous break-ins in our
area and beyond. This information seems to have the same effect
as the statistics provided me by another policeman in June. A car
is stolen every two minutes in the District of Columbia, I
learned. This was told to me as consolation for the temporary
loss of my beloved Toyota Cressida, named, by me, Troilus.

Sybil tells a detective who visits her later in the day that it
would be good if Seventh Street were better patrolled by police
cars. He agrees but reminds her that it is not possible for the
already overstrained police force to monitor all the business
streets. We smile at this. Two months ago we were visited by a
city inspector. He gave us a five-hundred-dollar ticket. It seemed
that our little A-frame, four-foot-high billboard placed outside
our door within an iron-grated area, containing literary
quotations, was a danger to public safety. Seventy customers
voluntarily signed a statement addressed to the District of
Columbia protesting the fine. They said the billboard was an
asset to the street, the city, and to learning.

Sybil had to take an afternoon off to appeal the ticket. The
judge was sympathetic and somewhat amused by the inspector's
avidity. He reduced the fine to fifty dollars, but told her the sign
would have to be removed. This she did, being afraid to court
further bureaucratic action. At the same time she removed the
small BOOKS sign that protruded a foot from the building and
nailed it flat against the window frame. Today we decided to
install a costly but necessary alarm system, and a grate for the
front window.

My partner is far more philosophical than I, who tend to
grow more and more paranoid as I live in the District and feel I

can count on the city only for senseless harassment, not protection. She tells me my fears of attack and mugging are interior, without reference to exterior events, unjustified by the statistics on crime in our section of the city.

I smile as I listen to her, not reassured in the least. *Interior?* For some reason, disconnected from what has happened, but evoked by the word, I remember the time I went to a funeral home to order a coffin for my grandmother. The funeral director was unctuous. He called the coffin a casket, and then asked if I wished a vault. 'What for?' I wanted to know. He was full of scientific information. He assured me, the loving survivor, that the steel structure 'would impede decay of the body' from attack by outside insect attack. I asked him if it was not true that the body was more likely to decay from the interior. He waved away this possibility. I waived the purchase of the vault.

So, despite police statistics, I feel at bay, attacked from within, sure that every passing young black is a threat. I despise the racism involved in this. How can I conquer it? Leave Washington for a while until my sanity and balance are restored?

October

This morning I visited my dentist, a wonderful fellow named Ted Fields who works on teeth during the day and spends all his free time in the evenings and on weekends in his studio doing witty and original ceramic sculpture. To get to his office on Nineteenth Street I pass a beautiful old building, three brick stories that wrap around the corner. It is now occupied by the World Wildlife Federation.

Every time I go by the place I am struck by painful nostalgia. Except for dental visits three times a year I find I avoid 1244 Nineteenth Street. In the front window, just left of the door, I sat for two and one-half.years, editing 'the back,' as it was called, of *The New Republic*. If every life contains one blessed time, no matter how short, a Camelot of the mind or spirit, these years were mine. I was fifty-four years old and alone, separated, by my decision, from everything I had known for thirty years—husband, job, city, apartment—and exhilarated by the sudden offer of the literary editorship of *The New Republic* in Washington, D.C.

To this day I wonder at Gilbert Harrison's choice of me. I

had no experience as an editor. After college and graduate
school I went to work as a title writer for
Metro-Goldwyn-Mayer (a job I obtained by simple nepotism,
my great-uncle being Marcus Loew, who owned the company).
After that, in quick succession, I worked for *Mademoiselle,* from
which I was fired for irreverence toward fashion copy, *The
Architectural Forum,* where I was a news writer, and *Time* in San
Francisco during the founding of the United Nations. That was
my 'experience.'

After two years in the Navy during World War II, I
'retired' to have children and write as a free-lance reviewer for
such Catholic publications as *America* and *Commonweal.* It was
in *Commonweal* that Reed Whittemore, then literary editor of
The New Republic, saw a piece of mine on Mary McCarthy, and
asked me to be a contributing editor.

I was amazed, and delighted. But I took the assignment
seriously, and went to Washington for a few editorial meetings.
Gil must have been surprised; in an off moment he had invited
me but, I suspect, never thought I would appear. Washington
was hundreds of miles from Albany. After a year, to my greater
amazement, I had that unexpected letter from him: 'My literary
editor, Reed Whittemore, has resigned to work on a book
about William Carlos Williams. Would you think about taking
the job?'

Good God! Would I! No offer had ever come at a better
time. Yet, very aware of my lack of qualifications, why did I
accept? I will never understand this. I was unwell during that
time, and the long trips (even driven by Sybil, my friend with
whom I planned to live) had been a strain. But Washington had
seemed to us, during our visits the year before, a striking city. I
remember Reed took us to the newly opened Kennedy Center
one night to see an Arthur Miller play. It was a balmy
December evening. During an intermission, Sybil and I stood on

the balcony looking over the dark Potomac with its sprinkling of river and shore lights. One of us, I don't remember now which, said: 'I could live in this city.'

So, despite the logistic problems of combining two households (she brought the furnishings of her house in Clarksville, I the remains of my apartment in Albany), we came to the capital, rented a house near a school for her two adolescent children, and began our lives together. After a few idyllic years at *The New Republic,* the literary editorship came apart. Her children left the city to live with their father; we bought a house together in a suburban part of the city called Barnaby Woods (there were noticeably few woods still standing). I went to teach at American University for ten years, while she went to work at the Library of Congress and, at almost the same time, opened the first of our bookstores in the basement of our house. We named it Wayward Books.

I said my editorship came apart. I meant to say: It was ripped to pieces by a long-bearded fellow named Martin Peretz who bought the magazine, making the usual promises to owner and editor Harrison that all would remain as it was. But of course, nothing in life ever remains as it was. (Sybil's useful aphorism for this phenomenon is 'Everything is different since it changed.') Peretz is a Rumpelstiltskin of a man with a volatile temper and inflexible convictions. Jewish affairs and the State of Israel were his passions. Gil was maneuvered out of the magazine he had turned over with such innocent faith and goodwill to Peretz. One day Gil departed, silently, telling no one. Soon after, either by Peretz's knife or resignation, others left in rapid succession: Stanley Karnow, Walter Pincus, Robert Myers, David Sanford, I.

That brief but lovely time was over. The weekly column I had written at the back of the book, called 'Fine Print,' ended. It reappeared for a time in the *Saturday Review.* When that

ill-fated publication slowly fell onto bad times, the column
disappeared entirely. Gil, a helpless gentleman before the furious
little man who had ousted him, retired to care for his ailing
wife, Anne, and, after her death, to write the biography of
Thornton Wilder. The rest of us went on to other things, Pincus
to a career as an investigative reporter at the *Washington Post,*
Karnow to fame with his books on Vietnam and the Philippines,
Sanford to a good job at the *Wall Street Journal,* I to teaching
and writing fiction.

Later, the title 'Fine Print' had a curious resurrection. In San
Francisco, at about the time the *Saturday Review* was bought yet
once again, there appeared a magazine devoted to the arts of
letterpress printing, called, most fittingly, *Fine Print.* At first I
felt litigious. Then I realized that only in the most personal way
did I own the title, and that this phoenix rise of the name was in
some sense fortuitous.

In Washington, in the next year, I met the editor of the new
Fine Print, Sandra Kirschenbaum. I told her of my interest in
printing and typography, binding and papermaking. Now I
contribute occasional reviews to *FP,* feeling at home under its
aegis. Once in a while I double-dip, as they say of writers who
use the same material in two different places, and review a fine
handmade book on the air. Yolla Bolly Press in California
printed a beautiful, expensive volume of John Muir's *Travels in
the Sierra.* I explained, in *Fine Print* and then on National Public
Radio, the pleasures of owning such a book. The response was
surprising. I mentioned the high price. Twenty-five people
called the publisher to inquire about purchasing it. Clearly, there
is a small but avid market for books that appeal to the touch, the
eye, the mind, especially in the presence of the fifty thousand
ugly, mass-produced, carelessly or tastelessly designed books that
pour out of offset presses and 'perfect' (not an accurately
descriptive term) binding machines every year.

∽

I read the obituaries in the *New York Times* this morning,
looking for the the tragic, telltale signs of an AIDS death:
young age, twenty-one to forty-five, the announcement of
death by a longtime companion, and the list of survivors,
parents, sisters and brothers, nieces and nephews. I sit still as I
find two such announcements today, the black pall of despair
coming over me for the others I loved. . . . Then I go on reading
on the same page. A writer, in her fifties, has died. I note the
judgmental power of the order of words, as well as the choice of
articles, the difference between 'Mary Fitz, a novelist' and 'the
novelist Mary Fitz.'

∽

For my birthday this summer, Sybil gave me a computerized
catalogue of my ballet books. It is a useful, handy present,
because once the collection exceeded two hundred volumes, I
found I sometimes bought the same book twice. I keep the
books together in the guest room, and find myself going there
often to browse. Today I read a rather poorly written but still
informative biography of Anna Pavlova, whose greatest role
was the dying swan. The pictures of her in action make it hard
for me to believe she was as perfect as she is described. But I
learn that as she was dying, she called her attendant and said,
'Prepare my swan costume.' The author does not say, but I
assume it was brought to her and Pavlova was buried in it.

∽

It is cold today. The leaves are yellow and blow about
underfoot and cover the flower beds. Trees begin to have their
barren, almost nude winter look. I wear my wool jacket to walk
to the bookstore to bring Sybil some late-afternoon coffee. I

decide to go into the long, red-brick Eastern Market to avoid
the wind. It is a pleasant walk-through. I know many of the
merchants. The chicken salesman named Melvin is an ardent
Redskins fan and wears the team's colors under his white apron.
Mr. Miller, of the deli, is in his eighties. He wears a fedora
while he works and brags that he roasts the beef himself. It is
beautifully rare. I don't have the heart to tell him his hand is too
heavy with the garlic for my taste. But Sybil likes it this way.

The cheese man offers me samples I would love to try,
except that delicacy is no longer permitted to enter my
cholesterol-laden arteries. The older lady with dyed-black hair
at the bakery has brought in her paintings-by-the-number to
display. She only reads paperback books by Jewish authors or
about Jewish life. The bakery counter is near the side door of
the market. I buy two blueberry muffins from her, admire her
art work, and leave the building reluctantly: It has grown darker
and colder. I walk quickly to Wayward Books, and deposit the
coffee on Sybil's desk.

We drink, and eat our muffins. On the sign blackboard, now
residing indoors near the door because of the foolish city
ordinance, is a Henry James sentence: 'It takes a good deal of
history to produce a little literature.' I ponder it. Is this what I
am doing here, dredging up masses of personal history in the
hope of producing a modicum of literature?

Now it is quite dark outside. The schoolyard across the street
is empty of its usual complement of basketball players. I decide
to wait until closing time at seven so I can walk home with
Sybil. I sit on the stool and pick up a volume of short stories by
a young man I knew briefly in the seventies. But I get no farther
than his picture on the back flyleaf. I see it was taken by Thomas
Victor.

Thomas Victor. He was an acquaintance who died recently
of AIDS, a fine photographer of writers. My friend Joe

Caldwell, the novelist, told me that Tom would ask his subjects
if they had any special likes or dislikes when being
photographed. 'Oh, no,' they would always say, 'anything you
want to do.' 'And then,' Tom told Joe, 'they would fight me all
the way.'

I remember Tom darting around the New York Public
Library to take pictures of notables at an American Book Award
gathering, a small, dark man with a perpetual smile, now gone,
his immortality a mere byline under other people's faces.

At seven-fifteen the cash is added up, the day sheet finished,
the alarm system activated, the door locked, and we start the
short, cold walk home. All the way home I think about Tom
Victor, which leads me into remembering that Joe Caldwell,
then a small boy, asked his grandfather if he could have his
books when he died. His grandfather said: 'Who's going to die?'

∽

We eat late, whatever can be cooked in a rushed half hour, and
'clean up.' Sybil is the perennial dishwasher, I the dryer and
put-awayer. She likes to wash, although she is firm in the belief
that the act of dishwashing ruins her hands. She wears rubber
gloves, which inevitably stretch. Recently she acquired a new
pair but adamantly refused to throw away the old ones.

'What are you saving them for?' I ask. Hoarder that she is,
she says: 'You never know when you might need a small piece
of rubber to stretch over something.' I challenge her to give me
an example of such a need. She is silent and goes on doggedly
scrubbing a pan.

Suddenly I recall my mother and me walking along the east
bank of the Hudson River on Riverside Drive. She watches the
boats moving in stately fashion up the river toward Ben
Marsden's Amusement Park in the Palisades, a place I loved. My
father used to offer to take us there on Sunday. (He was a man

given to making lavish promises, few of which he ever fulfilled. I believe he thought the offer was an adequate substitute for carrying them out.) I, perhaps eight or nine years old, always watched the eddies close to the shore, absorbed in their varied and sometimes puzzling contents, so much more interesting than the featureless flow of the cleaner water beyond. I see a strange sight, an extended, light-colored length of rubber floating limply in the wrack.

'What is that thing?' I ask my mother.

She looks to where I am pointing, flushes, and quickly looks away.

'That . . . that is a bandage you wear . . . when you have . . . a sore thumb.'

I remember we walked on. I watched the water intently and saw more bandages. It occurred to me that there must be an inordinate number of persons in New York City with sore thumbs. But I say nothing—until this moment, when I break my silence and say to Sybil:

'I've thought of a use. Condoms for considerate gentlemen.'

'*Also,*' she says, and finishes the dishes, clad in her tight new rubber gloves.

෴

Saturday. This morning, so absolute is my addiction, I find myself turning to the crossword puzzle in the *Times* even before I read the headlines. One clue is PALEY. The answer turned out to be, of course, GRACE. I remember the day when the clue was BOYLE, the answer KAY. This is true fame, I thought, to have one's name immortalized in a game that two million persons puzzle over while they drink their morning coffee.

When she appeared in my puzzle that day, I sent Kay a postcard, congratulating her on this recognition. She wrote back that several other persons around the country had written to her about her inclusion, some even sending the whole puzzle so she could see for herself. Then she effectively humbled me:

'I hope you are not one of those persons who does crossword puzzles.' As I remember I did not reply to this. Should I feel ashamed? Is this a lowbrow, unworthy occupation?

∽

A letter in the mail this morning from Jay Booth, a student friend in New Smyrna Beach, Florida. She says she has embarked on a new three-hour exercise program on the boardwalk in Dunes Park, a wonderful place that offers fine views of the sea. 'However,' she says, 'When I sit down to write, I fall asleep.'

This result of physical activity does not discourage her, she says. Because 'this year my literary prize blossomed. Two years ago I was awarded a dogwood tree for the first chapter of my novel, *One Fine Day*. As dogwoods do not flourish or even survive here, I thought the whole business ominous, also comical. Well, the tree flourishes. The book, on the other hand, is out to publishers. I have two rejections so far.'

∽

Correspondence has begun to arrive from the American Ballet Theatre about a projected two weeks in Paris, to live the high life, visit places not usually open to the ordinary traveler, and see a lot of ballet and opera. Jane Emerson, my daughter, is one of the organizers; I feel a certain maternal obligation to subscribe to the trip, but also some natural eagerness to see Paris again.

This evening I call to tell Jane I would like to go with her and her husband. Bob answers the phone. Jane is still at work at ABT, making arrangements. I ask him if he would find it onerous to be accompanied by an aging mother-in-law. He says, politely, not at all, he has a number of eccentric relatives. He once told me about his Uncle Seth, a man of absolute fidelity. After his first wife died, very young, he remained a good and faithful friend to her sisters and their many children. Late in life he remarried, having finally overcome his fidelity to his wife's memory. The new wife turned out to be psychotic; she was, apparently, treated by lobotomy. The son born to them was severely retarded. Now in his eighties, Uncle Seth concerns himself solely with the constant, loyal care of his wife and son.

I tell Bob to inform Jane I intend to accompany them to Paris.

∽

A letter from Ted and Robert, Washingtonians transplanted to central Maine, friends we made through the bookstore; they were among our early customers. They invite us to spend Christmas with them in Blue Hill while, they hope, we will look for a house to buy near there. Their friend Bill Petry, a real estate agent, knows of some places we might like to inspect.

Maine? *Maine?* Well, yes. Sybil and I have often thought about moving there, debating our separate and often contrary needs. I want to leave this dangerous, badly run, threatening, crack-and-crime-filled city. She loves the variety and excitement of Seventh Street, and the people who come in to Wayward Books to chat with and buy from her. Break-ins and violence happen everywhere, she says, citing the thug who broke into Ted's car when it was left overnight in a motel parking lot in Portland, Maine. In *Maine?* she wonders.

'Omaha, Nebraska, I have read,' she says, 'is a major terminus for the drug trade.' She reminds me that two years ago an anonymous caller had threatened, by telephone, to come and rape me in Iowa City, and that my rented house in that city was broken into through a side door on Halloween. But I continue

to remember my trashed car, and the sight of the floor of the
bookstore strewn with books and papers after someone had
ransacked it looking for the cash box.

I hate the sense of vulnerability I have on Capitol Hill, the
feeling that my grey head and unsteady gait make me a natural
prey of young marauders during the day, and especially at night,
when I have to park the car some distance from our front door
and make my hesitant, wary way across the dark street and
through the even darker path to the door.

Maine seems to me to be healthier, safer, cleaner, freer from
drugs, guns, muggers, gangs. This morning the *Post* reported an
eleven-year-old boy in Washington had killed his father, shot
off the top of his head with the father's handgun. The *Post*
called this an 'incident.' I am always shocked by the implication
of insignificance of that word. For some reason, the third and
fifth dictionary definitions are what I always think of: '3)
something that occurs casually in connection with something
else,' and '5) an occurrence of seemingly minor importance.' The
'occurrence' reported by the *Post* is more than an incident.

∽

This morning I sent my yearly contribution to the *Catholic
Worker,* a publication I have read and subscribed to since the
early thirties. My check has grown larger with time. I remember
my first donation was one dollar when Dorothy Day asked for
an emergency sum for the maintenance of the Catholic Worker
House on Christie Street.

Since then, during the years of my acquaintance with
Dorothy, and after her death, I have been one of those
conscientious but characterless supporters who gives money but
not themselves. Once, in the thirties, I worked in the soup
kitchen at Christie Street, and later on the coffee-serving line for
a longshoremen's strike. But those were youthful acts, 'incidents'

in a long, selfish life away from the slight service of my youth. Dorothy Day did it for me, offering her entire life for the poor, the homeless, the drunken and mad, the objectors to war, the victims of injustice.

My check, I remind myself, is not tax-exempt. I rummage in my files to find a copy of the issue of the *Worker* that contains the policy statement on this matter:

> We have never sought tax-exempt status since we are convinced that justice and the works of mercy should be acts of conscience which come at a personal sacrifice, without governmental approval, regulation, or reward. . . . Also, since much of what we do might be considered 'political,' in the sense that we strive to question, challenge, and confront our present society and many of its structures and values, some would deem us technically ineligible for tax-deductible, charitable status.

I admire this position. I have always cringed at the letters that arrive in December from charitable organizations urging me to contribute before the end of the year so I may take advantage of a tax deduction. The *Catholic Worker*'s statement reminds me of how much must be spent, in time and resources, to obtain and maintain a tax-exempt status.

I went to Dorothy Day's funeral a few years ago. It was a wonderful reunion of friends and former workers as well as present inhabitants and workers at the houses on East First Street and Maryhouse. Mass was formal and old-fashioned, the kind Dorothy loved and hated to see reformed. How ironic, I remember thinking as I watched the Cardinal of New York kneeling before her plain pine box, that a women who spent her life fighting for social reform and against the retrogressive social failures of the Church would not countenance any changes in the liturgy. But at the last, the hierarchy of the diocese came in full red regalia to the scruffy Lower East Side church to pray with the people she had cared for and officialdom had often turned its back upon.

'Works of mercy should be acts of conscience . . .' I seal the letter with my check and stamp it with a commemorative stamp that reads LOVE.

❧

October 10. I put down this date, although my habit in journals is not to do so. If something is worth recording, I have always thought, it ought to be general enough to be free of dull, diurnal notation. But this day:

I take the very early Metroliner (six-fifty, an unusual hour for me to take a train) to New York for a meeting of the board of the National Book Critics Circle, a group I have belonged to for many years. A law has been passed which, I believe, makes this the last year of my term, so I am determined to attend every meeting, despite the cost of travel. We are reimbursed only for the two last meetings in the year if we do not serve an institution that pays our way. National Public Radio does not do this for me.

We talk about NBCC business and possible recommendations of books deserving of nomination for an award. It is always fun to meet with other critics and editors. We hole up on the third floor of the Algonquin Hotel, and argue, insult each other pleasantly by challenging the validity of views different from our own, eat a buffet lunch together as we work, and take notes on books of interest we have missed and ought now to read.

At four o'clock the meeting is over. I planned to meet my daughter Jane at the Public Library for a cocktail party a publisher is giving to celebrate the appearance of the first volume of T. S. Eliot's letters. I need coffee, as I always do between events. Caffeine acts as oil with which to shift gears, sustenance for my flagging spirits. Flagging: why is that adjective always used for spirits? The *Oxford English Dictionary* informs me that the usage is three hundred years old and first referred to falling down through feebleness. It then was used for the heart, then the circulation. Matthew Arnold was the first to speak of 'a spiritual flagging.' I buy coffee in a plastic cup and carry it to the benches on Forty-fourth Street and Sixth Avenue (now called, grandly, the Avenue of the Americas, but in my youth known simply by its common number).

While I drink I watch a street lady eating a hot dog on a roll. Behind her and across Sixth Avenue is the store from which her food must have come. There is a huge sign over the door which reads: AMERICA'S 24 HOUR HOST. STEAK'N' EGGS. She converses with herself between bites in a loud, harsh voice and shakes her head at what I assume are the answers she hears in the air.

Her hair is composed of switches pinned, it seems, to a wig base, and at the top there is a great heavy bun. Her eyebrows are crusted and red, the same flush that covers her light-brown skin and culminates in an angry red ball at the end of her nose. Her body is very thin under a coat composed, like her hair, of parts that are pinned together, but her thinness disappears at her neck, which is full of thick folds of skin, like the necklaces African women wear to elongate their necks for beauty.

She finishes her hot dog, rises slowly, and walks to the trash container near the door to the office building. She moves as if her steps were painful. Her face suggests misery and resentment, as though the weight of all the bunches of cloth tacked on to her were depressing her spirits. She returns to her bench. Her profile is Flemish: the long, thin nose, the chin that falls away, a large black mole on her cheek. She wipes her mouth and her nose on her fingers and then puts them in her mouth. I shudder.

I finish my coffee, stand up to walk to the trash container, and, inexplicably, fall on my face. There is pain in my right ankle that turned and caused me to fall, and greater pain in my left shoulder, so intense that I cannot get up. I lie there, seeing two sets of feet in well-shined shoes pass me by without breaking stride. I try to think of a strategy that will get me on my feet, but without the use of my left arm and hand nothing works.

Then I see a brown hand near my face and hear the street lady's rough voice say: 'Here. Hold on here.'

I do as she says, doubling my arm against hers and gripping her loose flesh as she holds mine. She pulls hard, I hold tight, I am up, dizzy. She puts her arm around my shoulders and puts me down on the bench. She sits beside me.

The next hour I remember with disbelief. The street lady, Nancy, and I talked about her life while she inquired about my pain and dizziness and advised me about therapy. 'Don't get up yet,' she said, 'or you'll conk out.' I think about finding a telephone to tell my daughter, who might still be at work at the Ballet Society, to meet me here instead of in front of the library. Is there a telephone in this office building? I ask her. 'Yes,' she says, 'but whatever you do don't use it. The AT and T puts devils on the wires and they get into your ears.' I give up my idea of calling Jane for fear of offending Nancy.

She tells me that she has money to buy a winter coat but storekeepers won't let her try their coats on. Silently I determine to come back and find her, take her to a store for a coat, try it on, and then let her buy it. She tells me she went through high school, took an 'industrial' course, got a good job, married, had a daughter who lives now in another part of the city. 'She never comes by to see me. I don't know her address.'

In the same year she lost both her husband and her job 'and never could get ahead again.' She shares a room in a welfare hotel on Forty-sixth Street with three other women; they sleep in one bed in shifts. In warm weather she prefers to bed down in the doorways of her street, where the mattress devils can't get at her. And the evil spirits in the pillows. 'But I like to have an address. Welfare checks come to me there. So I have some little to get by on,' she tells me.

'Winter is the worst,' she says. 'Even now, in October, it's too cold.' Her parents came from Haiti, she says with some pride. Her mother told her she never was warm once she got here. 'But she saw I went to high, and then she died from her lungs and I married a bum, a devil.'

Five-thirty. I get up with difficulty. 'I'll walk with you,' she says, but I say no, I can make it now. I thank her and give her a hug and tell her I hope to get back to New York soon and then I will look her up at her hotel. She says, 'Oh yeah. Watch out for that devil at the front door. She's into voodoo and hexing.' I say I will, and limp down Forty-second Street to find an Ace bandage for my swollen ankle.

My daughter takes me to her apartment and then, this morning, to the Ballet's orthopedic fellow. He says my shoulder is broken, gives me pills and a sling and a warning to do therapeutic exercises after a week or else suffer permanent stiffness. I resolve to do as he says. But already, in all the night's pain and the next day's scurry to be relieved by a doctor and medicine, the memory of Nancy seems less distinct. Will I look her up if I come to New York at the end of the month for the Ballet's trip to Paris? Probably not, knowing how such resolves usually end for me.

∽

Despite the uselessness of my left arm, and the blue-black color of my shoulder, I decide I will go to Paris as planned. I suggest to Nora Kerr that I do a piece for the travel section of the *New York Times* to be called, tentatively, 'Paris on Five Hundred

Dollars a Day,' because the itinerary sent me by the American Ballet Theatre is full of luxurious events such as I have never experienced. The clothes I will need will cost a fortune, in my scale of things. I will need to retire my jeans and sneakers (women do not customarily wear pants in Paris, my daughter informs me) and acquire the proper clothing for the cocktail receptions at the U.S. Embassy, cocktails at Claude and Sidney Picasso's apartment, a cocktail reception at the Baron and Baroness Guy de Rothschild's, evenings at the Paris Opéra, the ballet, the theater, and concerts, a trip to Épernay for lunch with the Count Ghislain de Vogue, and, for the Friends of the Ballet I will be traveling with I suspect, the highlight: attendance at *haute couture* openings of Christian Dior and Christian Lacroix. Showings! Galas! Late suppers with royalty! Why am I, scruffy Doris Grumbach, traveling in this fashion?

I think of my usual mode of vacationing. I cram into an L. L. Bean duffel bag three T-shirts, two pair of jeans and two of Bermuda shorts, two bathing suits, snorkeling equipment (I have a mask that has lasted for twenty years and is entirely outdated but still serves me quite well), jungle bug juice, high-numbered suntan lotion, sneakers aerated by open seams in the canvas, and four or five hefty paperbacks related more to good intentions than to the realities of accomplishment. Last winter, for Kailuum in the Yucatán, I was accompanied by Thomas Flanagan's *The Tenants of Time,* the second *Rumpole Omnibus* by John Mortimer, and Kenneth Lynn's biography of Ernest Hemingway. What with the lack of electricity—I have often wondered how Abraham Lincoln managed to read for and pass the bar in Illinois with only the help of candlelight from dusk on—and the lethargy induced by constant sun, sea, sand, and snorkeling, I read none of them.

Now, with the prospect of an *haut monde* voyage to France even my luggage fails close scrutiny, not only the suitcases I resurrect from the storage place in the garage, now a little damp and moldy, but also my clothes. From inside to outerwear, they are inadequate. I have no 'dressy' dresses (this was my mother's word. She would ask of an occasion, 'Is it dressy?'), no suitable coat for evenings, none, for that matter for during the day. All my mother's vocabulary comes back to me: 'good' cloth coat, dresses that will pack but not 'muss,' shoes 'dyed to match,' beaded evening bag.

One of my daughters, Kate, a physician to whom such concerns are commonplace, tells me that I need a good Chanel suit for daytime wear, decorated in the new fashion with much gilt jewelry. Another daughter mentions Ultrasuede, a material I have not heard of before, as good for a coat or a suit. I feel depressed by the idea of modish clothing. If, at great cost, I acquire such a wardrobe, will it not be too late? Will I live long enough to wear it all on other occasions? Knows God.

∽

Jane sends me a list of prospective attendees of the trip to Paris, all supporters and devotees of the American Ballet Theatre. I know no one on it except for Jane and Bob, but I note with amusement that one of the active participants has an extraordinary first name: Bambi. It matches the current vogue for foolish feminine-ending names in Washington society: Muffie, Tammy, Cokey.

∽

This morning I worked at the bookstore. Sybil went to a book sale and our manager had the day off. On Sybil's desk, during a long pause from customers, I find an old issue of *Poetry* from 1964. It lists 'new' poets to the magazine, none of whom I have heard of, except for Stevie Smith. One of her poems I rather like, called 'Here lies . . .'

Here lies a poet who could not write
His soul runs screaming thru the night,
'Oh give me paper, give me pen,
And I will very soon begin.'

Poor soul. Keep silent. In Death's clime
There's no pen, paper, notion—& no time.

Writers agonize so about not being able to write, 'blocked' away from their Muse. Looking back a quarter of a century at *Poetry,* I see how futile much of our suffering is. We struggle to write what we feel compelled to, we believe we have something to say to the world. Twenty-five years later we are dead, our name is forgotten, our work, if it is noticed at all, is acknowledged with condescension and scorn. Why do we care now? I find I do not really know.

~

In the District, lottery fever is high. In Pennsylvania, the winning ticket will gain the lucky holder almost twelve million dollars. Someone from Sybil's office at the Library of Congress is driving to the state border today to stand on line for hours to get tickets for everyone in his section, including Sybil. I do not buy a ticket because I have no faith in the possibility of winning, even though I know someone will win. This morning the newspaper carries a column by a professor of actuarial science at the Wharton Business School (a line of work I had not realized carried with it a professorship) who has made some witty computations of events more likely to happen than hitting the jackpot with a single ticket. Among the events: 'You will live past the age of 114. . . . Your neighbor will commit suicide this afternoon. . . . You will play Russian roulette (one chamber in six containing a bullet) eighty-eight times and survive.'

I am firmer than ever in my conviction that it is absurd to invest any money in a lottery ticket at odds that are 9.6 million to one. I don't think Sybil expects to win. She enjoys the fantasy about what she would do with the money if she did, and is willing to pay money regularly in order to be able to sustain the dream.

∽

I am absorbed by García Márquez's *Love in the Time of Cholera*. When a novel I am reading grips me, I immediately analyze its sentences, not its plot or characters. I want to know how this magic, this transmutation from dead paper and print to live scenes and breathing persons, has been accomplished, like a child who asks of a magician: 'How did you do that?' I examine the words. Sometimes the answer lies in one wondrously selected and placed verb or adjective that, by itself, lifts a humdrum sentence out of its ordinariness and into startling, vitalizing reality.

Flaubert knew about this power of *le mot juste* to fire the reader. He made me aware, as well, of the force of the perfectly chosen metaphor. I learned from his 'maggoty moles' and I understood Emma's 'desires, her sorrows, her experience of sensuality, her evergreen illusions,' from the simile 'like a flower nourished by manure and by the rain.'

This everlasting search for how it is done slows me as I read, and what is not so good seems to insinuate itself into my writing. I try out the solutions to someone else's successful choices, and of course they do not work as well for me. I have to find my own way, like the wayfarer in Stephen Crane's poem who found the path to truth lined with knifelike weeds and mumbled: 'Doubtless there are other roads.'

∽

End of October: I have been to, and returned from, Paris, a most glamorous and expensive trip, yet full of visits to places I

might not otherwise, in my lifetime, have made, as well as
return visits to old, fondly remembered places:

• A fashion showing by one Christian Lacroix, of whom,
as you might expect, I had never heard before this trip. He
was described to me as 'the hottest couturier' at the moment.
I was not so much surprised by the clothes, which I had
expected to be wild and imaginative and colorful (having
seen the costumes he designed for the ballet *Gaîté Parisienne*
the night before) as I was by the models. Perhaps it was because
they paraded on a raised walkway, so that we needed to crane
our necks to see them, that they all looked at least six feet tall,
wonderfully sleek and slender, very solemn and serious about
what has always seemed to me to be the frivolous business of
displaying clothes. One of the most beautiful, I thought, had
shining grey hair and a very young face.

A woman seated beside me was taking notes in a
stenographer's pad. I assumed she was a fashion reporter (she
was) and she told me the glamorous, grey-haired model was the
designer's 'muse.' 'More than, er, inspiration?' I asked. She
seemed shocked at my ignorance. 'Well, I certainly assume so,'
she said.

• From my floor-length windows at the Hôtel Vendôme, I
could see the statue of Napoleon in the *place*. He wears a
Roman toga greened over by time, conceived and cast in this
curious form by Gustave Courbet in 1871. An enormous
144-foot metal shaft, made of melted-down cannon from
Napoleonic campaigns, lifts the Corsican into the sky. He looks
oddly small up there, diminished by the extent of his own
transformed artillery.

• Jane, Bob, and I deliver tickets for the evening's events
to the Intercontinental, the Ritz, the Westminster, the
Crillon, the Bristol, the Paris Athenée, all within walking
distance of each other, all full of similar gold, gilt, crystal,

marble, and shining mahogany lobby furnishings. Without the signs at the door I decided I could not have distinguished among them.

• I needed Kleenex (even in fall in Paris I have some form of hay fever), not provided in the little closet of a room I occupied at the Hôtel Vendôme. I found it for $3.50 a box. If one's cold hung on in this expensive city, one could go bankrupt.

• Bob and I walked to Sainte Chapelle on the Ile de la Cité, I clinging to his arm for fear of stumbling on the uneven, ripped-up sidewalks, concerned about my broken shoulder. An extraordinary display of stained glass on every side and stretching many stories high; even on this cloudy day the light through those spectacular windows is incredible.

• The Paris Opéra: 'The last hurrah of Second Empire opulence,' as the guidebook says, it surely is. Flying stone horses, ornate friezes, a copper cupola of Apollo holding a lyre above his head, Greek classical sculpture accompanied by baroque decoration, huge bowls of fresh flowers and thousands of well-placed lights and spotlights: the great wedding-cake, block-square structure is more exciting and glamorous than the static, stagy *Rigoletto* that we heard the first evening. For Christmas one year Rod MacLeish gave me a fine nineteenth-century photograph of the building, which now hangs in my living room. Michelin divides his guidebook to Paris into Quarters: the one containing the Palais Garnier is called 'The Opéra Quarter.'

• Bob and I entered the Louvre through a back door and walked through gallery after gallery of Chardins. Never have I seen so many dreary paintings on one walk through a museum's galleries. But we wanted to make our way to the new I. M. Pei entrance, still a month or so away from being opened. It is a curious pyramidal shape, to my eyes a likable structure, full of visible wires and struts, reminiscent in a way of something Buckminster Fuller might have designed. Since the Louvre itself is a great series of buildings covered over, *buried* under, baroque decoration, it was refreshing, even amusing, to see the entrance to it so simple and stripped-down that its very bones show.

• A lavish luncheon at the offices, studio, and showrooms of a Parisian jeweler, Alexandre Reza, a stocky, confident, perpetually smiling man whose father had been a jeweler in Russia. His wife, who works with him, is younger, slender, blonde, tall, and conspicuously undecorated by his wares. Six years ago, he told me, he 'stepped down to the street,' having sold his work before only from his workrooms. He said he becomes enamored of each stone he buys and talks to it as he prepares to give it its proper setting, tempting me to ask him if ever he thought to try to teach it to talk, as in Annie Dillard's anecdote. His settings are always gold, his stones he often buys from royal families, he speaks of his products as 'important pieces.' To my mind, his prices are astronomical.

'Do you ever make less costly pieces?' I asked.

'Surely,' he said. 'One day, a lady came in asking for something to wear to the grocery store—something simple. I was able to oblige.' In fear and trembling, I inquired: 'How much was it?'

'Ten thousand dollars.'

The small, raised windows of his shop on the Place Vendôme (closed to the public during the three hours of the luncheon) have been specially designed with ballet shoes and programs studded with elaborate matched pieces of jewelry. We are told they were done for our visit and will be dismounted as soon as we leave. Jane, an expert in these matters, estimates the cost of this affair—pâté de foie gras, salmon on toast, Beluga caviar in pancakes, salad, petits fours, a fine wine with each course, 130-proof Russian vodka with the caviar—was probably a hundred dollars a person.

'Don't worry,' she comforts me. 'One purchase will repay the cost.'

When I thank Monsieur Reza for the extraordinary lunch, he invites me to come back the next day to see his workrooms, a tour that had been promised for the whole group this day but had not fit into the schedule. The rooms are on the top floor of his building, reached by a very secure grated elevator. In a series of spaces, craftsmen sit, hunched over their delicate work, small, intense lights focused on their hands, the sloping gambrel roof seeming to push them even further into their seats. Under their feet is a latticed floor which, it was explained to me, prevents a stone or a small piece of gold from rolling very far. The whole scene was Dickensian. I saw some art books on the tables and realized that they were the source of many of Reza's designs, both of animals and the replicas of jewelry from old paintings.

Later that evening he sends around to my hotel an elegant satin evening bag, with his card of thanks for my visit. I am astonished, but brought back to reality by recognizing that it is not that he expects me to return as a customer but that he has heard I am going to write a piece for the *New York Times*. The couturier showing, the Reza luncheon, a glance at my hotel bill, the tab at the pharmacy, other incidentals, have supplied me with evidence for the article 'Paris on Five Hundred Dollars a Day.'

∽

At breakfast in the Hôtel Vendôme I shared a table with a pleasant-faced, very short and stout lady who was traveling with her son. He appeared to be in his late fifties or early sixties, a

quiet, kindly lawyer who treated his mother with great courtesy
and respect. I asked them how they came to be with the group
accompanying the Ballet.

She smiled broadly, her worn blue eyes lighting up. 'I was a
ballerina, with the Chicago Ballet,' she said. Her son regarded
her proudly. She pulled from her voluminous purse press
clippings and pictures of herself, Helene Samuels as she was then
called, in various poses, a slim, lithe, very small dancer with
lovely legs.

We ate our brioches and drank coffee in silence. I tried hard
to see in this serene, heavy old lady the prima ballerina of the
early twenties. *Sic transit* . . . But she displayed none of the
sorrow at the way things go that I was feeling. Cheerful and
gallant, with her son's attentive help, she rose heavily and
walked from the breakfast room very slowly, holding his arm. I
noticed that her legs now curved inward, her toes close, in a sad
reversal of Beauchamp's classic first position.

Another day I encountered Isabel Brown, also traveling, as
someone's guest, with the Friends of the American Ballet group.
She told me who she was: the former principal dancer with the
company (she seems now to be about fifty) and the mother of
three children who dance or danced with it—son Evan,
daughter Elizabeth, now no longer a member, and Lesley
Browne, now performing with the company in Paris as soloist.
My interest in this familial talent must have been apparent. She
told me about her career at length, pointing out with much
pride (and, I thought, a tight smile at my ignorance) that the
movie with Baryshnikov, *The Turning Point,* was based on her
life, that Lesley Browne (the name had somehow acquired an *e*
in the second generation) played her mother.

Isabel Brown is still slim and moves with the easy grace of
her profession. Only her face shows her age. She is fortunate in
being able to soften what must have been her unhappiness at

growing older and having to retire by her pride in her children. It must be hard to end one's career long before middle age because the most vulnerable part of oneself, the body, can no longer perform the requirements of the art. Ballerinas have inordinately short careers. They endure as long as their hips will allow for abnormal extensions of the leg and foot, as long as their toes hold their bodies aloft. Then they must retire to seats in the orchestra to watch younger women perform their roles. From star to spectator: it must be a difficult descent.

∽

In the Parisian dampness my shoulder stiffened up, and I began to worry about whether I would be able to swim well again. I confided my concern to Bob. We talked about the pleasures of snorkeling in the Caribbean as we walked two blocks in the rain to dinner at Le Lotti on the rue de Castiglione. He tells me about a couple he watched arrive at their cabin on a beach in Rhode Island. They unloaded a great deal of gear: life preservers, underwater cameras, snorkels, fins, masks, wet suits, hand weights. The weather was fine for the week they had the cottage. Bob never saw them leave their porch until the day they loaded all the stuff back into the trunk of their car. Readiness is all, he concluded. I could not make out whether he intended this anecdote to be comforting or not.

∽

I am a traveler who never thinks of persons I have left behind. So I spent my last day in Paris scurrying around the shops to find last-minute, ill-considered presents for friends and children. (No, *not* children, the foolish way I still refer to my daughters, all of whom are approaching or well over forty. *Women,* who are now, fortunately, my friends.) I made one stop at the great, ugly Romanesque Madeleine church. It was vast and empty.

The pew I knelt in smelled of fresh urine. I didn't move but stayed instead among the minor unpleasantness to pray for Richard, who is now close to death. Amid all the lavish display of the past two weeks, his suffering stands in clear contrast. 'Holy Mary, mother of God, pray for him now and at the hour of his death.'

∽

Marguerite Yourcenar: 'If you can say "mad with joy" you should be able to say "wise with grief." ' On the flight home I pondered the truth of this. I have seen many deaths recently, in so short a time. Yet I think I grow more foolish, not wiser, in my grief, with each one. I believed I was going home to Richard's death. The thought reduced me to weary tears. The man next to me asked if I felt all right. I said I did.

For the flight home I saved a pocket-sized volume of Montaigne's *Essays.* I spent most of the time reading one, 'On Certain Verses of Virgil.' Five pages into it, the flight attendant put dinner down over the book I had rested on the tray table, as though Montaigne were not there. Rude, I thought. As rudely, I suppose it must have seemed to her, I superimposed Montaigne over the aluminum-wrapped 'hurried' chicken, as it was referred to by my seatmate, who confided in me his deep dislike of microwave cooking. I did not open the aluminum foil to try the curried chicken. From experience (we'd been offered the same dish on the flight over) I knew it would be inedible.

How often the retired Montaigne's views of aging and old age and mine resemble each other's. We are both, like so many other persons in the four hundred years between his life and mine, much concerned with the changes from youth to age, with the miseries of aging, with the coming of death. But think: He was not yet sixty when he published the last edition of the

Essays, his only book, one he wrote (like Whitman) over and over again.

> In my youth I had need to admonish myself and look carefully after myself, to keep me to my duty; good spirits and health do not consist so well, they say, with serious and wise reflections. I am now in a different condition; the accompaniments of old age admonish me only too much, teach me wisdom, and preach to me. From excess of gaiety I have fallen into the more irksome excess of gravity.

He writes (at fifty-seven!) of what he regards as the failing of his old age, one I know, from having read the pages that precede this in my journal of the seventieth (plague) year, that I share:

> I am at present only too sober, too pondering, and too mature; my years daily instruct me in insensibility and temperance. This body shuns and fears irregularity. . . . not for a single hour, sleeping or waking, does it leave me at rest from teaching about death, endurance and repentance.

Montaigne's view of bad days are mine:

> Formerly I used to mark dull and gloomy days as unusual; these are now the usual ones for me, the unusual are those that are fine and cloudless. I am ready to jump for joy as for an unwonted blessing when nothing pains me.

Probably he was one of the first of the 'free' (as he terms it), honest and entirely outspoken confessional writers (after St. Augustine). To withhold the unpleasant truths of his character and his life seemed to him the worst possible sin:

> The worst of my actions and conditions does not seem to me so vile as I find vile and cowardly the not daring to avow it.

Just before I put up my reading table and return my undisturbed dinner to the flight attendant, I read:

> I have determined to dare to say everything that I dare do, and I dislike thoughts even that are not fit to publish.

Strange, to encounter again, and accept wholly, the relevant thoughts of a sixteenth-century philosopher as I cross hemispheres in a Boeing 747 airplane, while rejecting sustenance prepared in three minutes in a microwave oven. Things and methods change, often for the worse, valuable ideas remain the same, or grow richer. . . . The flight landed uneventfully, and we were thrust back abruptly into the 'new world' of American English, dollars, customs, and reverence for youth and physical beauty.

November

 W ashington is cold and windy, remnants of fall leaves still
blow along the dusty streets on the Hill, and my carriage-house
study is a refuge from the sounds of helicopters searching out
criminals in the southeast and sirens rushing to fires. My
daughter, Barbara, calls to ask about the Paris trip. At the end of
the conversation I find myself beginning a narrative I have
already told her. Horrified, I withdraw as inobtrusively as I can
and say goodbye.

Repetition: Why is it the elderly tell their stories again and
again, in the same company, to the same person? Forgetfulness? I
suppose. Finally, a limited supply of stories? The need to hold
up one's end of conversations? I have caught myself, too many
times, in mid-narrative, realizing, by suddenly noticing the
inattention in my companion's eyes, that she has heard this
before. Embarrassed, I search for a way out, a phrase that will
excuse my tedious rehearsal of events. 'As I told you before' or
'I know I've said this already, but . . .' and then I seek
desperately for some new material to add to the old story.

∽

A long, thin box arrives by United Parcel Service. I had
forgotten that Richard Lucas told me he had fallen in London
when he went abroad in July for Wimbledon. He had bought a
cane, 'a nice one,' he said, 'made of ash and wonderfully light,'
to help him to get to the courts.

'Now my legs are failing me,' he told me when he called
from California in September.

'Oh, I know,' I fill in awkwardly. 'I turned my ankle this
winter and fell and broke my shoulder.'

'Well then,' he said, with what sounded like delight, 'I know
what I want to send you. A cane like mine.'

The cane is fawn-colored and delicate, ends in a black rubber
tip, and still has the natural marks of the tree on it. At the top it
curves gracefully. Just below its turning point there is an
engraved gold band which reads: 'By Appointment/To H.M.
Queen Elizabeth/The Queen Mother/Umbrella Makers/Swaine
Adeney Brigg/and Sons Limited.'

The card says: 'Love Richard.' No comma. I love Richard, I
mourn the loss of function in his legs, I cry as I stroke the
smooth, lovely surface of my clone to his cane. I know he is
near death and, once again, as I have for the others I cared about,
I rail against the terrible injustice of his premature end.

I take my new cane and walk through the alley beside the
carriage house, cross Independence Avenue to Seventh Street to
Provisions, where I buy two coffees and two pieces of coffee
cake 'to go' (a truncated phrase I find ugly). I continue my
walk, swinging the cane, to Wayward Books. Sybil is glad to
have the coffee to keep her awake during the hours she must still
'man' the store, and very pleased at the idea of my using a cane.
'Oh, Richard,' I think, 'would it were you walking with it.' My

throat aches at the thought. I can see in Sybil's face the same unspoken sorrow.

∽

Today, *twice,* modern technology has failed me. I called a local hospital to protest a bill I have already paid. *Before* the mammogram pictures were even taken, I had been required to write a check. Nonetheless, the hospital's computer insists I owe the hospital money. I will wait for my check to be returned by the bank. . . .

And then, the bank! At noon I stood on line waiting my turn for a simple transaction. I needed to know the state of my checking account. 'Not today,' I was told. 'The computer is down.' Of course, this is nothing new. It has happened in other places—a department-store business office, a newspaper subscription department. My view of computers has become jaundiced. I left the bank feeling like a disgruntled curmudgeon, if that is not a tautology.

Driving home I suddenly was put in mind of Sister Joseph Clare, the registrar at the College of Saint Rose, where I taught in the sixties.

The college's enrollment was small and homogeneous, about nine hundred Catholic young women. Its faculty was drawn heavily from members of the founding order, the Sisters of St. Joseph of Carondelet. A few 'lay persons,' as we were called, filled positions for which no nuns had been 'developed.' Theology and philosophy were taught by three priests. The staff and administration were all 'religious.' (The vocabulary quoted is that of official Church nomenclature.)

Sister Joseph Clare was a college administrator. A pale, small, unsmiling woman, she was so slight that she seemed to disappear into her voluminous black habit. She occupied a narrow office lined with filing cabinets. At one end, under the window, was her small desk containing a pristine blotter on which I rarely saw any accumulation of papers. On one corner stood a plaster statue of St. Joseph, and before it a low vase of always fresh flowers. St. Joseph held his carpenter's tools in his hand. He was her patron saint. She, like him, was a tireless worker.

The college's record-keeping system had been devised by Sister Joseph Clare. It was simplicity itself. When a student registered, she filled out a 9 × 12 yellow card, ruled down the center front and back, a quarter designed for each year. Grades were handed in by instructors on long white sheets she had typed up with the names of students, a column to enter absences, another for grades, and a space for 'Comments (if any).' She noted the grade and course number on the student's card, and placed it in its proper place in a file cabinet labeled for that year. At the end of four years, she would record, in her minuscule, neat handwriting, the date of graduation, grade-point average, class standing, and honors received (if any). The record was regarded as complete when (as inevitably she did) she received news of the student's marriage. The new name would be entered in brackets beneath the maiden name.

Once, while I was on the evening faculty in the late fifties, I was in her office when a portly, middle-aged woman came in. Sister looked up from her desk, smiled, and said:

'Well, Margaret-Mary O'Donnell. Class of, let me see now, '47? Yes, I believe so. You married, I remember. It's now Margaret-Mary Kelly. How nice to see you again. What can I do for you?'

Visibly taken aback to find she had what she must have thought was a unique place in Sister Joseph Clare's memory, Margaret-Mary O'Donnell Kelly stammered out her request for a copy of her transcript. She was planning to apply to the State

University at Albany for entrance into its Master of Teaching program.

'Yes,' said Sister. She rose from her desk, with the sort of flowing motion that only nuns in full habits are able to effect, and went directly to the drawer of a file cabinet at the other end of the room. Without hesitation, she pulled a card from the drawer and brought it to her desk. In five minutes—perhaps less—she had copied the material from the card onto a piece of typewriter paper, signed it, stamped it with the seal of the college, and handed it to Mrs. Kelly.

'There you are,' she said. 'That will be fifty cents, please.'

Mrs. Kelly thanked her, paid the money, and left. Until Sister Joseph Clare died of what the nuns always called 'a wasting disease,' she retained her prodigious memory for the records of the College of Saint Rose. Never, as far as I knew, did her retrieval system fail her.

In the years that followed her untimely death (that is a clichéd, foolish phrase. All death is untimely except one entered into by one's own hand), a downstairs classroom under her office was converted into a computer center. If the machines down there in any way resemble those in banks, hospitals, and libraries, I am willing to wager they are often down or out. I have a suggestion for IBM about this state of affairs: I think it ought to abandon its manufacture of computers and start developing nuns.

ᔢ

Sybil and I go to Great Falls across the river in Virginia for our last, winter look at the rushing water and violent swirling eddies, inhabited even this late in the year by devoted kayakers. The falling water is wild and beautiful. The leaves on each side of the Potomac are red, gold, brown, yellow. We stand at a lookout point beside two teenage girls.

One says: 'I saw a doe drinking at the edge as I climbed up here. And of course I forgot to bring my camera.'

The other: 'Too bad. Let's go. What's there to see up here?'

∾

At the end of the stairs in my study I have posted a memory sheet, to remind me that I must pay attention to the tyranny of machines and other devices. It reads:

TURN OFF PC/Printer/Surge Control/Lights/Coffee
          Maker/Overhead Fan/Thermostat
TURN ON   Answering Machine/Outside Light

When I get to the house the unwritten but no less demanding list is: TURN OFF outside light/oven/stove gas jets/power to VCR/television/radio/fans/air conditioners in bedroom and kitchen, *und so weiter*. At the time I bought these things, or installed them, they were intended to add to our comfort and ease in living. Now they have mounted up, to the point that we do not ride on them, as Thoreau said of the railroads he disliked, they ride on us. I try to take a stand against still another of them by steadfastly refusing the gift of a microwave oven someone wishes to give us. Sybil believes the instant, or almost instant, cooker will improve the quality of our suppers, so I will probably give in, add 'TURN OFF microwave' to my list, and sink deeper under the Rule of the Machine.

∾

I am reading a collection of John Cheever's letters, edited by his son. They are wonderful. Cheever wanted his correspondents to destroy his letters. 'Saving a letter is like trying to preserve a kiss,' he said. Fortunately few did. 'I am much less afraid of burglars when I am busy,' he wrote. When last did I hear the word 'burglar'? It has begun to sound old-fashioned. Now we talk about muggers, break-in crooks, thieves. A burglar has the ring of Conan Doyle and Poe: archaic. Cheever's language gives these honest, sometimes painfully revealing letters a curiously decorous sound.

∽

I am sent in the mail a glossy magazine, thick almost as a Sears catalogue, called *Museum and Arts*. It is published in Washington. There is a slip in it that says it is being sent to me because I am mentioned in it. Snare. Trap. Hook. I go carefully through the damned thing, reading here and there, when I can bear its fancy, overheated writing and unreal colored photographs, and of course, I am not. I realize I have been suckered into wasting an hour in an egotistic search for myself.

∽

An editorialist on the radio begins his lecture with 'A thought I want to share with you.' 'Share', of course, is not what he means. Listen to me, he is insisting. There is not the slightest chance that you can reply. 'Share' is a misused verb these days.

∽

Back from Paris for some weeks, I find I often think of those exciting days and nights. Reliving a trip is an added virtue of travel, just as preparing for it is sometimes better than the journey itself. (Sybil's delight is more often in the planning stage. The actuality for her often falls short of expectation, which nothing, of course, can diminish.) To my surprise, looking back, it was very good to have the company of the Emersons. Indeed, my well-being depended on them (a reliance I have always resented in my early years). Bob took my arm through all the always-being-repaired streets of Paris; Jane helped me bathe and dress. Hooking one's bra is an impossibility with a broken shoulder.

> MARK TWAIN: 'I have found out there ain't no surer way to find out whether you like people or hate them, than to travel with them' (Tom Sawyer's observation when he goes *Abroad,* 1894).

Traveling alone is curious. One experiences new things more directly but quickly tires of it when one has no one to tell about it. William Hazlitt thought otherwise: 'One of the pleasantest things in the world is going on a journey; but I like to go by myself.'

I remember one January in the late sixties in London, when I was preparing to write a biography of Mary McCarthy. I found the month at first a welcome escape from the constant presence of family and the world of academe. But after a week of frigid, raw streets and a cold desk in the library of the British Museum, solitary poor meals, good but lonely teas, walks, queues, theaters so cold I had to wear gloves through all the performances, I grew tired of myself, and then of the city, and then of Hazlitt's vaunted pleasure in solitary travel.

$\backsim$

The Sunday *New York Times,* here at six in the morning, to stay the week until I can absorb the essays in the magazine, do the puzzle and the Double-Crostic, read the travel, entertainment, and 'Week in Review' sections; I am always at least a week behind in the 'Week in Review.' But I read the *Book Review* first, and note that Faith Sale, the editor whose judgment I questioned last spring, now has a worthy best-seller, Amy Tan's moving and original *The Joy Luck Club.* Last winter in New York, after her publisher's party during the National Book Critics Circle affairs, Faith pressed upon me the galleys of Tan's book. I read it on the Metroliner going down to Washington, and loved every gentle, graceful word of it.

Later I see in the *Times* that its paperback rights have been sold to Vintage for $1.2 million and I rejoice. For once the rare event, a good book appears on the best-seller list among all the adventure tales, mysteries, romances, science fiction, horror, and popular schlock. The author will make money, a great deal of money, it seems, and the editor will be celebrated at her house and all around publishing for her astuteness in acquiring such a good novel, and a first novel at that. For once, all's well in this narrow corner of the publishing world.

ᔫ

'There is no pain greater than being bitten by one's own dog.' I remember this astute sentence but cannot for the life of me remember who said it. Mark Twain, it may be.

ᔫ

I am back at work culling material for this memoir from my notebook of last summer. At Peggy Danielson's house in East Blue Hill, where I tried to bury all thoughts of my seventieth birthday, I found a prayer the sculptor Lenore Straus had used to conclude her book on the process of creating a stone statue, now standing in Norway:

> O God,
> hold my hand
> that
> holds the tool.

Without using those precise words, I often find myself praying similarly before I sit down with my clipboard. Substitute 'pen' for 'tool.'

Peggy told me that in the last few days of Lenore's life, when she was dying of cancer, she worked on tiny wax sculptures. Much reduced in size from her customary larger-than-life heads, these little figures contrasted significantly with her heroic stones, signifying not just the diminution in her energies but her sense of how little was left to her life. Never once, having been compelled almost to give up her hold on life, did she abandon her art.

Louise Nevelson (in a book on her work by Arnold Glimcher): 'In the end, as you grow older, your life is your art, and you are alone with it.'

In a book on Zen Peggy gave me, I found Lenore's AA card: 'Anonymity is the spiritual foundation of all our teaching, ever reminding us to place principle before personalities.' Useful admonition, not only to the alcoholic but also to the book reviewer.

Reading *Nevelson* I come upon another statement by the sculptor: 'You have a white, virginal piece of canvas that is the world of purity.' I expected she would add that the artist proceeds to pollute or pervert or degrade it by painting on it, but no. 'And then,' she writes, 'you put your imprint on it, and you try to bring it back to the original purity.'

And then she says: 'My work is delicate; it may look strong, but it is delicate. True. Strength is delicate.'

∽

'Have a good time,' someone says to me, hearing I am going away for the weekend. 'Let's have a good time tonight, and eat out,' I say to Sybil. 'A good time was had by all' is the way social items end in little local newspapers in small towns. Good time. Ford Madox Ford wrote in *New York Is Not America* (1927): 'It [New York] is the city of the Good Time—and the Good Time is there so sacred that you may be excused anything you do in searching for it.'

I put into the storage bin of my head some new lingo I have just come upon in a novel about Las Vegas. In gambling, 'drop' is the total amount bid at a gambling table, 'cage' is the place you cash in your winning chips, the 'pit boss' is the executive in charge of a group of gaming tables during a work shift. And best of all, 'toke'—a tip given dealers by a patron. One never knows when it will be necessary to use one or another of these words, in life or in fiction. They are fine Anglo-Saxon, monosyllabic words, good to have in place of elaborate modern pseudoscientific jargon.

I remember the pleasure I felt as a college student when I discovered the force of few words and the power of the monosyllable, that 'a minuscule edifice' was not as effective as 'a little shed.' In William Strunk's mimeographed sheets which I first encountered at Cornell I found the instruction 'Use definite, specific, concrete language,' and an example: For 'A period of unfavorable weather set in' he suggested 'It rained every day for a week.'

December

*O*nce again I mourn the change of season. Into winter now, I think of loss of light, of deterioration of trees and gardens, of letting go of sunlight and water to swim in. In a dour mood, I thought this morning while I waited for coffee to brew (always a low moment in my day) of the things I once wanted, and hoped to have in my life someday: a sailboat, a swimming pool, a convertible. Until last summer when, feeling the ineluctable pressure of age, I recognized that these dreams will not materialize. May Sarton once wrote to me: 'What is it I can have that I still want?' My version of this is more direct. What I once wanted, I know now I shall not, ever, have.

∽

I've been rereading Annie Dillard's *Pilgrim at Tinker Creek* and find I have marked in the margin:

> I am the arrow shaft, carved along my length by unexpected lights and gashes from the very sky, and this book [*Pilgrim*] is the straying trail of blood.

That is what this memoir is: a straying trail of blood, with not much optimism that it will dry up and disappear, or turn to Hansel's white bread crumbs that will lead the reader out of the black forest into light and hope.

∽

Today I heard a name, of someone older than I. It often happens to me. The name may be of a poet, an actor, a public figure from the past. I think: He must surely be dead because *I* have not heard or seen that name for a long time. Can he still be alive? Surprise. Then, pleasure. He has survived my ignorance of his existence.

∽

Beginning of a dark month of despondency. I am working on *Camp,* a novella about my thirteenth summer as an 'intermediate camper' (as we were called) at Crystal Lake Camp in the Catskill Mountains. It comes hard. When I see the light in the kitchen across the way, and know that Sybil is home from the bookstore and puttering around with food for our late dinner, I want to leave the carriage house and join her. But I'm not finished rewriting the section I am stuck in.

I know why people choose occupations that take them daily into offices, shops, faculty lounges, stores, and theaters. They prefer to be surrounded by other workers, conversing, exchanging observations about the news, last night's TV programs, weekend plans, family anecdotes, the everyday trivia that constitute life in the world.

People like me sit alone from early morning to midafternoon, sometimes later (like tonight), confined to one-way talk with lined paper and a yellow-on-black display screen, and then with a white page called, inelegantly, a printout. The telephone is turned off. We are engaged in a

one-way, solipsistic monologue. The sound of one's own voice
on the page grows tiresome; one runs out of things to say to
oneself. The house is silent, the Holy Ghost, reputed to be one
source of enlightenment, does not descend, the compost heap in
one's head stops 'working.' There is no one to complain to about
this sudden, inexplicable dearth of ideas.

After many years of such solitary confinement, I fantasize
about being younger again, coming to the job I once had in an
elegant townhouse on Nineteenth Street in Washington, D.C.,
walking to work in the fresh, bright, early-morning air carrying
three plastic cups of fragrant coffee and three sugar buns,
greeting Robert Myers and David Sanford, my friends at *The
New Republic,* sitting in my little office that looks out on the
washed street, eating, drinking coffee, planning, questioning,
joking, gossiping. There was a satisfyingly warm, intimate air in
the office, made up of the odors of recently showered and
powdered and shaved editors, fresh coffee, crisp, unread galley
sheets, and warm sugar buns. For the moment, in this place, at
this time, all is right with one's life.

∽

A warm early-December day. Sometimes December in
Washington can have just such unusual days. Once, when the
Modern Language Association was meeting here in the days
between Christmas and New Year's Day, we gave a small
luncheon party out on our deck for friends who were attending
the meetings. Everyone sat delightedly in the sun, in shirt sleeves
and cotton slacks. Someone even complained of the heat.

Today is reminiscent of that day, so warm I dream of spring
coming tomorrow without having to pass through the dreaded
winter. I take my clipboard across to the deck, and start to
outline a possible short story. (By 'possible' I mean there is a
slight chance that I will be able to bring it off.) Middle-aged

writer, a good writer with a very small but persistent (over many years) critical reputation. For each successive novel gets very small advances, wins an occasional obscure literary prize. Develops a block, bad block. In this sterile period, a very young (twenty-seven) writer is published. First novel. Acclaimed. Book-of-the-Month Club main selection, half-million-dollar paperback rights sale, foreign rights too, movie purchase, etc. The horror: He has the same name as the hero. Some common name, like John Smith, Joseph Brown. Not even the grace to add a middle initial. In one fell stroke, a 190-page novella, in fact, makes an instant killing. Even if his start is too fast, too early, like spontaneous combustion, he is so far ahead of his namesake, with that one stroke, that the hero will never catch up, never regain his hold on his own name. Too little time left for him, too little desire. His block. Gives up entirely. Changes his name and goes to work selling books for a chain in malls. Defeated not by success (as his namesake might well be) but by two proper nouns.

∽

I get only so far, and then find it hard to go further with the skeleton, to stretch on a Procrustean bed a tissue of words. Sometimes I am stopped by an outline that is too complete. I think it would be better, safer, to dive into the beginning of a story, not knowing where I am going, and let it bloom, blossom, proceed by budding.

I remember an opening sentence: 'He lived alone with a daughter who had died and a wife who had left him.' A startling opening, but so complete in itself that one would be unable to go a step beyond it.

Other times I have been blocked by plain lack of experience, a condition not easy to believe of a woman past seventy. But still, never once in those years have I been homeless, not one night in more than twenty-five thousand nights. I have never been hungry nor missed a single meal, except by choice. Never dirty for more than a few hours. Very rarely very sick: I have lost no limbs, no interior organs, not even appendix or tonsils or adenoids. I have never been abused or rejected or (as far as I know) mentally ill. I went to war, was in the U.S. Navy but was never allowed aboard a ship. All these avenues of experience, and a thousand others, were cut off for me. I feel the absence, even though I think I remember reading that Henry James was able to write a story about Huguenots after glimpsing a family of them seated around a table as he was going down the stairs past their apartment. But my compost heap lacks some essential nutrients. How can I write? I ask myself, put my pen into the metal tip of the clipboard, rest my head on the back of my chair, and settle for a suntan on the warm, unproductive deck. I know why I prefer writing out of doors. If nothing comes, if I am unable to write a word, there is still some gain: the sun on my skin, which, despite every medical warning, I still love and indulge.

〜

Recently, waiting in line for a book sale to open, I heard about the exercise program of a fellow buyer. She told me she and her friends drove regularly to a vast shopping mall in Virginia in the early morning before the shops within it open. They stride rapidly through the enclosed corridors. From one end to the other and back: a little less than a mile. If they are feeling energetic they walk the route twice.

I am aghast. In late November, to do some early-Christmas scouting for gifts, Sybil and I arrived at Tysons Corner a few minutes before ten. I tried to imagine taking daily exercise in those sterile halls, between walls of glass, stainless steel, and black protective gates, denied every natural odor of mossed tree trunks and pine cones or breezes from the sea, salt, fishy smells, wet dunes. I tried to breathe deeply only to inhale captive, stale whiffs of cigarette smoke, pizza and popcorn, sneakers and sweat suits, yesterday's coffee and french fries. The air is motionless, an artificial compound of synthetic odors. For me, a mall represents the essence of the eighties, a plastic chamber of horrors, reminiscent of the feeling in Sartre's play *No Exit,* devised for persons growing old in cities, shielded, for the moment, from polluted air, water, the failures of the ozone layer, and the damaging rays of the sun, and from the fresh morning of the spirit.

∽

The Library of Congress Reading Room, where I go on occasion to use its reference section, harbors some wonderful characters, so intriguing that often I am distracted from my work to watch them. There is a lady who calls herself the Bride of Christ. She dresses in white, surrounds her head with a thick white veil, and carries a wooden cross whenever she gets up from her seat to change her book. Passing behind her on the way to the card catalogue, I try to see what she is reading. I cannot tell; the book is upside down. Another middle-aged lady never takes her feet from the floor when she walks. She is called 'the glider' by the librarians. One can identify her passage without looking up by the long, swishing sounds as she moves about the room. I lunch with the librarian in charge of the reading room. Tori Hill is small, charming, tolerant, witty. She volunteers, an evening a month, to do the accounting work for Wayward Books. She tells me of a recent trouble. Yesterday a street person who spends the winter months in the reading room was found to be slamming his book on the lice he had picked from his hair. A number of such dead insects were then discovered in books he had used. She asked him to be de-loused before he returned. He was unwilling to leave. She was gently insistent. A guard guided him to the outside door.

↝

Dan Harvey, my old friend who is a distinguished publicist, calls to tell me that Richard died yesterday at home in San Rafael, California. I had spoken to him the day before. He was unable to answer me when his friend Zach put the phone to his ear. When I said I loved him and was thinking of him, I heard a low sound, like air forced from his throat and nothing else, but I believe he heard and understood me. I pray he did.

I have a vision of his gaunt face and white hair across the atrium of the Fogg Museum last year, where we met for the university presses' annual convention. A band is playing. Young, vigorous, smartly dressed press people are drinking champagne, eating shrimp, talking loudly, brightly, to each other. He is at the edge of the festivities, leaning against the wall, looking weary, but smiling to everyone who stops to speak to him.

We hug, kiss. I try not to feel the unfleshed boniness of his back, his shoulders, his thin arms under his elegant silk suit. Richard, my beloved friend, is now reduced to a little more than half the size of what he was. He asks me if I think he has changed. I love this man and yet I can do nothing, not the smallest thing, to help him or save him from this accursed plague except silently plead with him:

'Don't die.'

Out loud I answer his question: 'Only that you are thinner.'

Now he is gone, having entered what Freud called, in another context, 'the splendid isolation' of death. When I called him last month to thank him for my beautiful ash cane, he told me he had bought tickets for the Met's new production of the Ring. 'When is it?' I asked. 'Next April. Two tickets. Zach will come with me.' This was after his legs no longer served him. I marveled at his optimism. Wimbledon and opera are his two passions. I prayed he would make it to the Ring as he had to the tennis matches. But no. His own *Götterdämmerung* arrived first.

∽

On the same day, I read the obituary of the Reverend James Sandmire, who died in San Francisco at the age of fifty-nine, of AIDS. He left 'a longtime companion,' a daughter in Dallas, a son in Salt Lake City, a father and two sisters in Oklahoma, another in Utah. He was a Harvard graduate, an elder of the Universal Fellowship, and a founder of the Metropolitan Community Churches in San Francisco, 'which welcomed homosexuals.' He tried to affiliate his church with the National Council of Churches, telling them that 'the reason people come to our church is because they can't come to yours.' The National Council of Churches rejected his application.

∽

Christmas. Two days before, we left at six in the morning, and then waited almost two hours to leave the ground; the airport was crowded with planes in line before us. The plane to Portland came into fog, turned back to New Hampshire, landed, heard a new weather report, took off again, finally found a hole in the heavy bank of viscous cloud, and went down to land. We rented a car and made the four-hour drive north through heavy rain and, at the end, thick darkness that made it hard to find the road to East Blue Hill. It took us almost a day to come from Washington to central Maine.

But then we were at Bob and Ted's house in the woods. A huge fire burned in the oversized fireplace, dinner was almost ready, and Peggy, our hostess last summer for my dreaded seventieth birthday, came from her family dinner to have another dinner with us. We admired the tree that 'the boys,' as I foolishly call them (they are fifty-eight and forty-eight), decorated with moss, lichen, pine cones, and birch bark, and heard about their friend Bill, the real estate agent who wants to show us some houses in the area.

Next morning, firm in our resolve to look but not buy—after all, it is far too early for such a change; Sybil has at least two years before she can retire from the Library of Congress, and the lease on the bookstore is for another year—we set off in two cars to look at property. It was a crisp, cold day, ice on the paths. I walked holding Bob's arm. But the roads were amazingly clear, the air was bright, and sun shone on the black, bare limbs of trees. No one is about. The town's streets, stores (those few that remain open in the winter), and fields were all deserted. Our little caravan was the only occupant of the roads.

We looked at a number of places, large Maine houses with attached barns, a house high on a rise that looked out on the road before the bay, another buried in woods, one with 'a partial view,' which turned out to mean, in real estate parlance, that one could see the water in winter if one climbed to the second floor and squinted out of one window. Sybil is interested in proximity to a good road, in order to relocate Wayward Books someday; I want a generous view of the water, and complete privacy. Neither of us thought about immediate purchase and relocation. But we trudged from place to place, voicing our objections, almost glad that nothing suitable presented itself.

At one house, a former bed-and-breakfast, we met another agent who listened patiently to our dislikes and needs and then told Bill that he knew a place in Sargentville, down the road a bit, that we might like. Bill had not seen this place but still would take us there. Now we were a procession of three cars. Sybil rode with George, the new agent, Bob and Ted followed, Bill and I came behind.

We had just pulled into the driveway of the house and

stopped when I saw Sybil coming around from the front. Her face was flushed and she seemed to be breathing hard. I rolled down the window. She put her head into the car and said:

'I think we are in serious trouble.'

I got out and followed her. A little way around the stark, simple, undecorated house, we came upon a magnificent view, a cove at low tide. Beyond it was a strip of blue water, a deep-water mooring marked off by a crocodile-shaped strip of black rocks, and then two grey buildings far down the opposite shore. The grey hills of Deer Isle were in the distance. The view was constructed like a theatrical set, with diminishing coulisses extending to the rear. Over it all, winter-gaunt gulls rose and descended. The trees—an oak at one side of the cove, two spruces at the other—were barren or browned, the ground at our feet crisp and grey, like frozen shredded wheat, the uncut meadow beyond a low jungle of vines and what appeared to us to be weeds.

We were indeed lost. Without ever having set foot in the house, we knew instantly we wanted to live on this cove, in sight of all that varied, layered beauty and blue winter water. We went through the house, a place that had an adequate but not excessive number of rooms. One, a former summer kitchen, might be converted to a decent-sized study. Painting was needed everywhere, one chimney was broken down, another unlined, the roof needed work. We might add a deck from which to view the cove by day, the big sky by night, and a screened porch to avoid the annual April, May, and June mosquitoes and black flies, a somewhat different kitchen and bathroom, perhaps. But what was all that in the light of the glorious cove?

We went to lunch with Bill and, to our amazement, talked about a contract. The next day we signed one, containing an offer to be submitted to the owners, closed our eyes, and breathed deeply (Sybil admitted she felt sick to her stomach from the moment she put her name on the paper), overwhelmed

by what we had done so precipitately. We owned a house in
Washington we had to sell before we could buy this one, Sybil
had years to go before her planned retirement from the Library
of Congress. I was horrified by the prospect of moving five
thousand books and the contents of the North Carolina Avenue
house (the overloaded result of the consolidation of our two
households years ago) to Maine. By *May*. The closing on the
sale was set for late April.

How could we make sense, order, and progress out of all
this? We flew home in a state of shock, bewildered by what we
had done. A chaotic future stretched out before us, a jumble of
real estate dealings, cliff-hanging financial arrangements, and,
once again (five years after we had vowed we would never
move again, never go through those terrible months of
upheaval, restoration, and dislocation), all the slings and arrows
of settling into a new, strange place, fixing another house,
learning the vagaries of a capricious and, we had heard, most
difficult and lengthy winter, and acquiring, at our unlikely ages,
new acquaintances and friends.

A year ago I wrote in this memoir: 'It is too late now to live
in a new place.' Now I think: How dare I plan to live a life in
Maine in the dwindling time that remains ahead for me? The
joke is that people are now mentioning such absurd things to us
as a thirty-year mortgage. I remember when Jack Leggett, in the
summer of 1982, asked if I would like to come to the Iowa
Writers Workshop for a semester. I said, 'When?' He said, 'Oh
maybe, the spring of '84.'

I thought: How dare I think so far ahead, at my vulnerable
age? But now it seemed the older one grew, the less realistic one
was about the future. Even with all the dire anatomical
warnings that arrive on occasion, optimism rules one's decisions.
History serves my hopes. Once before, when I was fifty-four, I
left the life I had led for more than thirty years, my marriage,

my longtime tenured teaching job, everyone I knew, the city I had lived in or near for more than twenty years, and went off, like the youngest son in fairy tales, to seek my fortune, and another, different life.

But then I was younger or, I think now, young. Now I am old, having despairingly celebrated my seventieth birthday last summer. This should be the age of settled decorum, stability, even sedentary acceptance of what one has or is left with. How is it possible to change everything again? Will it work?

∽

Less than two weeks after our house is opened to the public (a violation hard to bear, but there is no other way to sell it but to 'show' it) there is a sale contract on it. The reality of what we have done bears down upon us. If we sell it at the price we have agreed to, there will be no mortgage on the Maine house. At this point I remember Sybil's utterance when first she saw the cove. Now she decides, when the time comes to live in it, that we should name the house Serious Trouble.

∽

Certain that we will be leaving this house on the Hill, it suddenly becomes dear to us. We stand on the deck we built, and watch the evening shadow of our one backyard tree, a lovely American elm we have nursed, fed, pruned, and venerated. Against the carriage house it makes a spare design, like a Japanese print. We listen to the water recycling in our minuscule pond and think of Lazarus, whom we forget to bring into the house this winter. He led a miraculous life in the pond, emerging from the slime that had formed into a frozen crust on the water, to show himself as grey-black and much thinner, but *alive,* resurrected, a sign of his faith in the arrival of spring. We watch bulbs emerging from the once bare spaces in the front garden and realize that after five years, it is finally shaped and filled in the way we hoped it would be. We remember its hazardous state five years ago when, in the weeks after we moved in, we discovered it was inhabited by the bravest stand of poison ivy on Capitol Hill. Banished after much work by gardeners, both of whom, in the process, contracted terrible cases of the rash, is the lethal growth. Soon, we, the conquerors, will be gone as well.

∽

I find written on the flyleaf of a book I bought yesterday:

> MARCUS AURELIUS: 'Look within. Let neither the peculiar quality of anything nor its value escape you.'

∽

We resolve to have framed and to take with us to Maine a pen-and-ink drawing of the facade of the house on North Carolina Avenue made a few years ago by a local artist. We believe we wish to be reminded of our contented years here. Sybil is depressed by the prospect of leaving. I am apprehensive about the future, but glad to abandon Washington, having grown less courageous in these past months about threats and mugging on the streets and robbery in our house and store, and our proximity to crack houses in the city. I am aware of my sensitivity to traffic noises, sirens, midnight cries of children in the house contiguous to ours, circling helicopters, passing airplanes.

∽

Yesterday I sat in the waiting room of the physician who is taking care of my slowly healing shoulder. Around me are elderly patients with casts on ankles, arms, necks, a few in wheelchairs accompanied by exasperated-looking middle-aged children. There is a look I have grown to recognize on the faces of captive offspring caring for parents they have long since ceased to love.

A white-gowned young blonde woman with the high, structured hairdo called a 'beehive' appears at the door of the waiting room and says:

'We're ready for you now, Lucy.'

One of the annoyed-looking men stands up and wheels 'Lucy,' who is clearly over eighty, through the door. He is carrying the pink slips that indicate 'Lucy' is a first-time patient.

I am in my customary state of fury. How dare that receptionist, surely not more than twenty years old, address the elderly woman by her first name. She has never met her before, knows nothing about her except that she is old, and sick. *Lucy!*

I sit there fuming, remembering a visit I made a few years ago to a nursing home on Wisconsin Avenue in Washington. My acquaintance, a professor emeritus of English literature, had broken her hip, and was here to recuperate. We talked for a while, about the study of Whitman by Paul Zweig she had been reading, about the new Marguerite Yourcenar I was reviewing. Then a young woman in white carrying a pail and mop came into the room, smiled brightly to the professor (whose doctoral work had been done, as I recall, at Oxford), and said:

'Hiya, Eda Lou. Don't mind me. I'll be out in a minute.'

Professor Morton shut her eyes.

'That's a good girl. Don't need to watch while I clean.'

I said: 'She is Dr. Morton, not Eda Lou.'

But the young woman, engrossed in her task, which took her through the middle of the professor's room but under nothing, seemed not to hear me. She finished quickly while I sat stonily and the professor lay with her eyes closed as if waiting for the final assault. It came as the young woman went out the door, calling behind her:

'Be good, Eda Lou. See ya tomorra.'

Let neither the peculiar quality of anything nor its value escape you. The peculiar quality of this encounter has stayed with me, sensitizing me to the indignity, in hospitals and nursing homes and waiting rooms, of reducing the elderly sick to children, ignoring the respect due their years and accomplishments, and the dignity of their adult titles or married names.

My turn comes for the orthopedic surgeon's attention.

'Ready for you now, Doris,' the woman with the beehive head says, the same bright smile on her face as the cleaning woman had in the nursing home, displaying her affected charm and familiarity with the patient.

This time I am ready. I do not move.

'Doris?' the young woman says, somewhat louder, suggesting by her tone that I, the only woman left in the room, must be deaf.

Aha, I think, I have her. She comes toward me, by now convinced I must be both deaf and, as we used to say, dumb.

'DORIS?' she shouts almost in my ear.

I stand up, forcing her to step back.

'Miss,' I say, 'I am Mrs. Grumbach. A stranger to you. About fifty years older than you, I would guess. Don't call me by my first name. What is *your* name, by the way?'

'Susan, er, I mean, Miss Lewis.'

To her credit, she blushes furiously, apologizes, and follows me into the doctor's office. 'Please be seated, Mrs. Grumbach,' she says. 'Dr. Moore will be with you in a moment.'

'Thank you, Miss Lewis,' I say. The war, of course, is still to be waged, but I have won this small skirmish. As it turns out, my shoulder appears to be better. Probably because the weight of my indignation has been lifted from it.

January

*W*ashington is dull, grey, damp, cold. I want to go to Mexico, as we often do at this time. Our reservations for air travel, and a week of tenting at Kailuum, are in place. But Sybil worries about being here for all the paperwork, inspections, etc. that will be involved in completing the sale of the house. My selfishness triumphs. *I* will go away at the end of the month, with Ted and Bob, who have never seen the ruins at Chichén Itzá and Uxmal, and then, if everything is finished in Washington, Sybil will join us at Kailuum.

∽

Does one grow more selfish as one ages? Clearly yes. I have said more times than I care to recall that now I will do nothing in my life that I do not want to do. Nothing. Ever again. Pure selfishness. Sybil bridles at this firm declaration but diplomatically says nothing.

A certain willfulness does not prevent me from talking about myself more than I would like, looking back in the evening at conversations during the day. My frame of reference has narrowed. I have become more Ptolemaic in my view of the world. Events and people surround me, I do not encircle them, along with everyone else. I remember: In the convent in Marian Engel's novel *The Glassy Sea,* the Eglantine Sisters are permitted mild conversation but are not allowed to talk about themselves. I would do well to practice this.

∾

Before I start to prepare for Mexico (thank God it is not for Paris; finding my mask, snorkel, and flippers and resurrecting old sneakers, shorts, and bathing suits will be the main tasks), I have been trying to work longer hours on *Camp.* The novella form is new to me. I find it hard. At moments I think the story ought to be expanded to a novel. At other times, I feel the desire to shrink it to a short story. This morning my impulse was to gather the printout pages, fold them neatly, tear them in half, and bestow them on the trash basket.

At moments like this, the meagerness of my imagination overcomes me. James Joyce is said to have written to an aspiring author: 'Young man, you have not enough chaos in you to write a novel.' Growing old, there is less chance of creative chaos. Or what there was was long ago smoothed out and reduced to orderliness by pedestrian prose.

∾

I am preparing to send my stack of notebooks, dating back to 1950, to the University of Virginia, together with other papers they are storing for me, on the slight chance that someday they will be of interest to someone. Idly I examine the notebook for 1981 that starts with a list of resolutions for the new year. It begins with 'Accustom myself to enjoying solitude.' The second is humorous, in the light of the past and the future: 'Grow thinner.' 3: 'Finish *The Magician's Girl.*' That one I managed to fulfill. 4. 'Work steadily on the Willa Cather book.' (Fitfully, it turned out, would be a better word. I am still at it, eight years later.) 5. 'Spend less.' Humbug. This never has happened, probably never will, until I am forced to do it by a drastic reduction of income. Otherwise, I will always spend a little more than I have. Number 6 was, is, a perpetual resolution: 'Practice my faith more regularly, more thoughtfully.' The list ends with: 'Simplify—my life, possessions, number of friends and acquaintances, emotional responses, food.'

At the back of the same notebook is the next year's list. Revisions have taken place. Number 7 has become 1 and says simply: 'Simplify.' Number 2 remains the same. Number 1 has slipped to 3, 6 has moved to 4. Number 5, for some enigmatic reason that must have had to do with an unproductive year, reads: 'Work.'

Making resolutions is an absurd but traditional rite of the New Year. This month, I've made a single, long, interrelated one: 'One more time, prepare to CHANGE. Do not regret the present. Do not fear the future. Adapt psychically to moving and difference.'

∽

Reading my old notebooks bores me. How dull and unimaginative I was, what foolish things I found to say about what I was reading and seeing. To restore my confidence in this sort of literary egocentricity I find on my shelf a book I have not looked at in years, Anton Chekhov's *Note-Book,* translated, interestingly enough, by May Sarton's friend S.S. Koteliansky and Leonard Woolf. Published in 1921, it contains a note by the publisher B.W. Huebsch explaining that it contains 'notes, themes, and sketches for works which Anton Chekhov intended to write.'

Now, I think, I will see what real, useful, suggestive,

interesting journal-keeping is like. In the introduction, Huebsch assures me these entries are 'characteristic of the methods of his [Chekhov's] artistic production.' I sit in the corner of the dining room in my new leather chair that tilts back, my feet on the matching leather hassock, and read through the book's almost 150 pages.

My disappointment is profound. Or perhaps it is my denseness in not being able to recognize the implications of these entries:

'On a Sunday morning in summer is heard the rumble of a carriage.'

'They say: "In the long run truth will triumph"; but it is untrue.'

'They fell upon the soft caviar greedily, and devoured it in a minute.'

'What a lot of idiots there are among ladies. People get so used to it that they do not notice it.'

'The parlormaid Nadya fell in love with an exterminator of bugs and black beetles.'

'He learned Swedish in order to study Ibsen, spent a lot of time and trouble, and suddenly realized that Ibsen is not important; he could not conceive what use he could now make of the Swedish language.'

These few samples are not selectively culled; I chose them at random. I could easily have included most of the entries. Note the last, curious one, about Ibsen. Surely Chekhov must have known that Ibsen wrote in Norwegian. A slip of the pen? Translator Koteliansky, clearly an admirer as most translators are of their subjects, suggests that it is a quotation, something C. overheard. He has simply omitted quotation marks. Hmm.

But my own notebooks are even more sterile. The surprise of Chekhov's pages is the curiously unproductive (to this reader's thinking), barren, *unrewarding* nature of the entries. What *could* he have made of them? Clearly he expected something, but of themselves they hardly seem worth puttting down. If I had come upon them in my notebooks I probably would have burned them. But Chekhov surely thought them capable of blooming. Huebsch says: 'The significance which Chekhov attributed to this material may be judged from the fact that he recopied most of it into a special copy book.'

I open up my notebook for this day and enter another typically plodding, forgettable sentence. 'Perfect name for an actress: Fay Wray.'

∽

A sudden memory flashback this morning when the mail brought a copy of *The Southern Review*. About ten years ago, I had a telephone call from Pamela Broughton at Louisiana State University. She wanted to know if I would wish to be considered for an appointment that involved editing *The Southern Review* and some teaching of literature. The term would be five to ten years. I said I would think about it and call her back.

I did think about it, about the weather in Baton Rouge in summer, about Sybil's dislike of the South as a place to buy books (our one experience of ordering books from a dealer in Miami resulted in a box that contained a liberal sprinkling of moldy ones), about leaving Washington for that length of time, about Sybil's antipathy to moving.

I did not get to call Professor Broughton back. She called me. Her voice rang with apology and remorse. It seems the chairman of the search committee had, in the interim, checked me out in *Who's Who in America* and discovered I was the same age as the man who was retiring.

'So,' she said, her voice very low under the weight of her embarrassment, 'I must ask you *not* to consider the appointment.'

'Fine,' I said. We hung up. I remember feeling relieved, but shocked. It must have been the first time that the full force of my age, sixty then, struck me. Too old to be something else, I remember thinking.

◠

Unpacking my snorkeling gear in the garage of the carriage house, I find an old bottle filled with sea glass. Since my first days at Moody Beach in Maine years ago, when the painter Marian Sharpe showed me specimens, I have been an avid collector of well-worn, unusually colored glass washed up and caught in the sea wrack. I am also always on the lookout for examples of perfect shells, stones (deceptively beautiful because they quickly lose their wonderful colors as they dry), odd pieces of driftwood (on the wall of my study I have a fine cross that must once have been part of a lobster pot), bits of porcelain that suggest seaborne breakfast sets washed overboard during a storm.

All my acquisitive instincts are awakened at the sea. After a walk I realize, to my dismay, that I have looked too little at the sea, too much at the sand at my feet. Tonight during dinner Sybil says that she has often wondered why this is so. She has observed, she says, that even the most sophisticated visitor to the sea becomes a greedy beachcomber. Why, I wonder, feeling a sudden pang of guilt. Avarice? Desire to 'bring something back,' like photographs, to remember a good time? Pleasure at finding 'something for nothing'? A desire to own and keep a piece of natural beauty?

We come up with no answers. I like the last suggestion, but then my idea of beauty would astonish someone like H. L.

Mencken who once observed that Americans are driven by 'a positive libido for ugliness.'

∽

Libby, the lady who owns the corner antique store on Seventh Street, is missing from her usual seat in the window. I inquire of her neighbor in the art store. She is in the hospital; the diagnosis is cancer, but they say they have 'caught it in time.' She will be all right. Such a statement is the bromide of medicine. We have all learned to recognize it as the doctors' consolatory, wishful thinking, the patients' desire to believe, the world's hedge against despair.

Libby is the very spit and image of Colette. Her hair is dyed blonde, curled, and cut short and springs away from her head, her skin is fine and pale, and the lines in her face are kindly, put there by smiling. The window of her store, her desk beyond, and the aisles and shelves behind that are models of disarray and disorder, dust and obscurity. Yet, from her chair, which she rarely seems to leave (like Colette), she sends the customer directly to the object requested, and with one gesture she finds in the confusion of her desk the paper she wants.

I miss her when I walk past her closed store. I say a prayer her affliction has indeed been caught in time, and that she will be back in her window, waving to me, a gentle, Colette-like salute to a passing admirer.

∽

The *Post* this morning: 96 DIE AT BRITISH SOCCER GAME. In the first paragraph the event is called an 'incident.' Another incident. Is 'tragedy,' I wonder, too heated, too vast a word for journalists?

∽

I stop for morning coffee at Provisions, a civilized shop across
from the Eastern Market that provides a small alley of tables,
chairs, and newspapers, for people like me, and Ted Nowick
when he is not in Maine, to take time out from work at home.
Two very pretty young women are at the table behind me. I
overhear their conversation.

'I feel rotten.'

'Why?'

'I'm menstruating.'

Times and language have changed, sometimes for the better.
I remember all the silly euphemisms we used years ago for that
universal feminine condition: 'I have my period.' 'I have the
curse.' 'I fell off the roof.' But we have not yet eliminated the
foolish evasions for urination and defecation. I still hear 'I have
to go to the little girls' (or little boys') room, the powder room,
to powder my nose.' 'I need to use the john.'

∽

Dan Harvey and Roger Straus (the Younger) hold a party to
remember Richard. I go to New York for it. My daughter
Barbara, who knew Richard slightly, and had driven me to
Oneonta to say goodbye to him in the fall, comes with me.

It was a most satisfying occasion. Dan's apartment is one of
those large sprawling old West Side places, which he has
beautifully restored. Guests came from publishing houses on
both coasts. Seminarian friends of Richard's came from all over.
I was the only representative of the College of Saint Rose days
in Albany when Richard (then a priest) and I taught there. We
ate, drank, and stood around in little clumps reminiscing about
him: his charm, his intelligence, his exceptional good looks, the
gallantry and grace of the end of his life. My cane. Someone

else's birthday gift, a box of California figs, which arrived the day after Richard died. The April Ring tickets.

A priest friend wondered: 'Who will use them?'

Another friend from the seminary years said: 'He will. One of them, anyway. The seats will only seem to be empty.'

∽

In my rereading of writers' journals on my shelves, I find in Katherine Mansfield's a note: 'Perhaps it does not so much matter what one loves in this world. But love something one must.' Katherine Anne Porter, in her essay on Mansfield, writes that this is 'a hopeless phrase. . . . It seems to me that St. Augustine knew the real truth of the matter: 'It doth make a difference whence cometh a man's joy.'

Reading the journals of others forces me to wonder how much truth ought to be included here. Even if I aim for what seems to me to be truth, will not the very process of putting it into words and setting it down fictionalize it? And then there is the natural reluctance to open all the sores and secret miseries of one's life, the misdoings and meannesses. Truman Capote would have required me to tell everything: 'No matter what passions compose them, all private worlds are good, they are never vulgar places.'

In print, I would prefer to appear better than I am. 'There is only one tragedy, that we are not saints'—Leon Bloy. I would like to feel I have used the materials of my life and the persons involved in them fairly, but of course I know I have not. Nietzsche, in his *Aphorisms:* 'The poet behaves shamelessly toward his experiences; he exploits them.'

If anyone should wish to write about me after I am dead (in case that *should* happen), will not the biographer try to find, buried under my euphemisms and charitable thoughts about myself, the true monster? James Boswell, I remember, said he would not change the nature of his beloved subject: 'I will not make my tiger a cat to please anybody.'

∽

A letter from a former student now teaching English in a high school in the South: 'I have gone back to trying to build vocabulary because they have none, or what they have is entirely street jargon. You will be amused. In one vocabulary test I received these: "Virtuosity: having many virtues" and "Trope: a traveling company of actors." '

∽

A sailing enthusiast in our store, looking for books on wooden ships, uses the phrase 'sail by the ash breeze.' I ask him what it means.

'Go at your own speed, without help.'

I once thought that was entirely possible. Now I know my speed is determined by failing limbs, weak ankles, loss of confidence. (Perhaps this is why I dream often about going down a flight of stairs so miraculously fast that my feet do not touch the steps.) As for progressing without help: no longer possible.

∽

The cleaning lady says the bathroom is now 'crazy clean.' She is sympathetic to my having to live in a two-story house. 'How you standing up to the stairs?' she inquires.

∽

Today I throw away the last pages of *Camp*. I'm not sure that will help the novella, but sometimes total elimination is more efficacious than rewriting the same thing over and over. I remember the painter Frank Litto, my friend in New Baltimore,

once told me that he was making creative use of erasure.
Reminded of Frank I go on to dredge up another phrase he used
once. He told me he was 'on the hanging committee' for an art
show in a new gallery that would include his work. Made him
sound like an active part of a posse or a lynch mob.

∽

At National Public Radio today to tape four book reviews, I
join a small group of employees who are talking about the death
of one of the directors. I notice that middle-aged persons react
according to sex at such news. Men ask: 'How old was he?'
Women: 'Of what?'

∽

Walking to the market—a freezing, raw morning—I see a very
old man ahead of me, holding on to the railings of successive
houses, scraping his feet in galoshes along the ice. From the back
he reminds me, for some reason, of Harry, my father-in-law,
whom I loved because he loved me, and because he had the kind
of sharply inquiring mind self-educated persons seem to possess.
He would get up at five in the morning to watch a program
they once ran on television called *Sunrise Semester.* Having left
public school in Brooklyn at the age of eleven to work in his
father's butcher shop, he wanted to read everything he could
find on social and political history. I remember he once called
me up to discuss a theory he had developed after reading a book
of Barbara Ward's for the TV course and was shocked to hear I
hadn't read it. He loved to argue, asked your opinion of a
matter, and then said he held the opposite view, which he
defended vigorously.

After many failures and disappointments in his lifetime—he
lost his long-held job as manager of a knitting mill when the
union came in and wanted him out, he drank a great deal, he

moved from Brooklyn to a small town in Pennsylvania where he never managed to make a go of his small knitting store—he settled into old age. He was cantankerous, still argumentative, still intellectually vigorous. He believed most of modern life was a hoax, a sting, a sham, assuring us all, when *The $64,000 Question,* a TV quiz program in the fifties, first appeared, that it was rigged. We all scoffed. It was.

He foresaw corruption in sports. Baseball was his life's passion. He predicted the dishonesty of some politicians in his time, and those he suspected turned out to have their hands in the public till.

How he knew these things I never understood, unless his knowledge sprang from a general distrust of the human race that happened, more often than not, to be entirely justified. But he was often a cheerful man and saved sentences he had heard in his shop to tell me when we spoke on the telephone on Sunday mornings.

My favorite, said by a lady who came in to buy wool: 'I would like to knit an African.'

∽

Mist outside the door this morning at six when I went to pick up the *Times* was grey-white and thin. It reminded me of the skimmed milk I now drink, in obedience to diet instructions.

∽

Tomorrow I leave for Cancún with Ted and Bob, to revisit the great Mayan cities I love. Sybil, staying behind to conclude the house sale, is clearly disappointed not to be going, but good-natured about it. To justify my defection I spent the evening beginning to pack the Mark Twain collection. After one box, I stopped halfway into the second one, having discovered a book I had forgotten I had. I found it in a small town outside of Iowa City a few years ago. It is *The New Guide of the Conversation in Portuguese and English* by Pedro Carolino, published in 1882 in Boston, and contains an ironic, tongue-in-cheek introduction by Mark Twain, who predicted 'pretty confidently . . . that this celebrated little phrase-book will never die while the English language lasts.' He compares 'its delicious unconscious ridiculousness and its enchanting naiveté' to 'Shakespeare's sublimities.'

He was right: 'One cannot open this book anywhere and not find richness.' I spent the rest of the evening in a chair, not packing but laughing and copying out samples of the English translations of Portuguese phrases, in fact the whole of Dialogue 17, about how 'To inform one'self of a person':

How is that gentilman who you did speak by and by?
Is a German.
I did think him Englishman.
He is of Saxony side.
He speak the french very well.

Tough he is German, he speak so much well italyan, french, spanish and english, that among the Italyans, they believe him Italyan, he speak the frenche as the Frenches himself. The Spanishesmen believe him Spanishing, and the Englishes, Englishman.
It is difficult to enjoy well so much several languages.

Twain, who loved to make fraudulent translations from the French and German, says of the final sentence: 'I am sure I should not find it difficult to enjoy well so many several language if he [Senhor Pedro Carolino] did the translating for me from the originals into his ostensible English.'

So much for packing.

༄

New acquisitions from two books I am reading, made to *my* vocabulary before I fall asleep, my bags in the hall downstairs ready for the trip to Mexico:

Sleepwort: the Anglo-Saxon word for lettuce.

A recovered word, which I once knew but had forgotten: Prolepsis: anticipation (in rhetoric, a figure of speech in which objections are anticipated). Adj: proleptic.

Psychasthenia: a neurotic condition characterized by obsessions, phobia, the like.

Anosognosia: defective body image. (Happens after a stroke when person does not believe in its results, denies paralysis, for example.)

Folie à deux: two persons (twins, perhaps) who develop shared delusions or become mentally ill at the same time.

I may never find a use for any of these, but they're nice to know. Maybe 'sleepwort' will fit somewhere, sometime. After all, Bill Kennedy used 'ironweed' profitably.

February

*A*fter Mexico. I have returned from two fine weeks in the sun, bringing with me no notes or entries into the journal I carried all those miles. At home I find a letter from a friend and former student, David Tate. He writes that he had gone to Spain to be restored after finishing a book. It worked. 'I think part of it was the opportunity to see fresh things and to stop thinking stale thoughts, to stop, for long periods, thinking at all, just looking, smelling, tasting, all the sensual delights I have been overlooking.'

Same here, as we used to say when I was young. I spent the first week at my beloved ruins, forgetting all the houses and possessions I have been worrying about, in Maine, on North Carolina Avenue, on Seventh Street. Suddenly there was nothing before my eyes but the grandeur of El Castillo looming skyward in the early-morning light, massive, stolid, grand. Of course I can no longer climb it, but no matter: I remember the view from the top and spend my time now memorizing the way it rises in geometrically diminishing layers, marred only by the little ants of people who are triumphantly scaling it.

In my new obsession with questions of death, I spent more
time than usual at the Platform of the Skulls, the Temple of the
Warriors, and the bloody frieze at the ball court. I was aware of
how much darker the glyphs and friezes had become from the
first time, fifty years ago, that I saw them. A fellow traveler told
me it is the result of pollution; soon the beautiful faces and
disembodied heads will be entirely obscured by black film.

During the sun-soaked days the site is filled with noisy
visitors. The Nunnery, the Governor's Palace, the cenote, lose
their mystery. But we went back in the early evening before
anyone else by an entrance customarily unused. The sun was
dying and the dreadful light show for tourists had not yet
started, We entered the Great Plain on a footpath. There it was,
a deserted city, the great grey stones, enigmatic and silent. A
holy place even to us irreverent twentieth-century travelers,
struck dumb before these ancient, inscrutable architectural
secrets.

My sense of mortality wells up in me, closing my throat, my
eyes, bowing my head. I am threatened by stone eternities. The
Mayans believed that man is already dead, awaiting only his
acceptance into the eternal life of the gods. Or else, in this life,
that man awaits death by joining his blood to the already stained
soil of sacrifice.

My friend, standing beside me, says: 'It gives one pause.'

I find this a good way to express one's awe. 'For in that sleep
of death/What dreams may come . . . Must give us pause.'

࿇

At the Temple of the Warriors, I saw vestiges of paint on the
pillars. They suggest the past glory of color that the now grey
stones have lost. So much is lost here beside color. We came
upon a tiny sign that read CHICHÉN VIEJO, pointing into the
jungle. Next morning we followed the path, so narrow that one

foot had to be placed directly in front of the other. Two miles of hard walking and we came upon overgrown, small, lovely vestiges of buildings, one with a rude upright fertility sculpture: A plump, uncircumcised phallus protruded from the half-fallen wall. Buried in high brush were two fine stelae carved with warrior heads, a truncated jaguar, other small carved stones. The recent Hurricane Gilbert had wrecked many of the old trees that lined the path. It is a forgotten place, clearly neglected by avid tourists and misinformed guides. We felt as though we had been presented with a small piece of antiquity for our private delectation, refreshing in its unrestored state.

Restoration is now the curse of the Mayan ruins. My daughter Kate and Paul Yarowsky, whom she is to marry this summer, told us to visit three small sites a short distance from Uxmal. We arrived very early at the first, Kabáh. It was entirely ours for almost two hours—a Puuc village, with many beautifully carved Chac masks on a two-story building, a superb corbel archway, standing alone, the sole survivor, I think, of a structure that now lies strewn across a little plain.

Robert Taylor and I felt a little like John Stephens and Frederick Catherwood, who first saw Chichén Itzá in the nineteenth century or, at least, first recorded their sight of it, until a busload of tourists arrived. We were alarmed, but needn't have been. They walked in one phalanx to the edge of the site, stared, took out their cameras (one to every tourist), snapped pictures of what they could see from that distance, turned back, got on the bus, and were driven away. Total visitation time: fifteen minutes.

But this is not what I started to say. At two other small but beautiful cities, Sayil and Labná, both of which had fine 'palaces,' corbel archways, and, at Labná, the remains of a mirador (observatory), there are crews of 'restorers' at work. Stones driven to the sites by pickup trucks are being slapped into position with white cement, so thick that in places it overwhelms the stones. There is no sign of any authority dictating where the stones should go, only a crude plan designed to make everything *appear* whole, and thus please what the Mexican government must expect to be an influx of visitors and their accompanying Mexican guides. These voluble chaps, in my experience, will spend their time profitably, creating ingenious fictions for their tour groups.

Returning to Uxmal after two days in the crowded Spanish city of Mérida was, for me, like returning to a cherished dream, one that comforts me when I awake from nightmares and think: How can I get back into last night's dream of a sunlit place? Uxmal is Maya's city of cities, with the finest buildings, the most carefully restored places, the most awe-inspiring views and vistas. After two days revisiting the places I love, we came back one last time in the early morning of our departure, before the buses from Mérida arrived. We each went our own way, having decided to have some time alone at the place we wanted to remember most clearly. I went to the Governor's Palace, and, as always happens there, I saw details I had not noticed before: the beautiful abstractions that the decorations on the great frieze create, the two perfect corbel arches, set into the building without a thought to symmetry, the clear, central Chac, the balustrade at the right which breaks mysteriously before the arch.

No one is quite certain what use the building was put to. Some say it was the residence of high holy men or 'governors.' Someone else suggests the great long corridors with many small rooms constituted places of civil business. If so, it must be the world's most beautiful office building.

I sat on the back of the stone jaguar who lies lazily before the palace, trying to store up behind my eyes every fine detail to sustain me until my next visit. Then I heard a familiar click. Cameras. Laughter. The guide rattling off, to a party of German tourists, his customary display of misinformation. No one seemed to be looking at the Governor's Palace except through the lenses of cameras. Three of the German women, substantial but healthy-looking, posed in a corbeled arch doorway and everyone took pictures of them. I left, and joined Ted and Bob, who had been driven off the Temple of the Dwarf by a similar influx. Their disturbance was in Italian. We said farewell to the beauty, the mystery, the awesome silence of the city of a people who inexplicably left their ceremonial grounds to the ignorant and insensitive mercies of tramping, talkative Europeans and Americans, as well as Mayan guides unashamedly distorting their own history.

In these temples, and perhaps under the hundreds of still uncovered mounds, there were the bodies of decorated and well-supplied priest-kings. I have read that a small piece of jade (the most precious possession of tenth-century Mayans) was placed in the mouths of the dead. Some say this was to guarantee their entry into heaven, others that jade was thought to be life-giving. The essence of the stone would be absorbed by the spirit of the dead to ensure his continued spiritual survival. A similar practice: ceremoniously punching holes in pottery buried with the dead to kill the vessel, reducing it to the same state as the dead.

But to assure the preservation of life after death: In the museum in Mexico City is a magnificent mask, made entirely of jade, which probably served to cover the face of a great chief buried in the Temple at Palenque. As we drove away, we debated whether to return to Palenque next year or to spend the time in polluted Mexico City. Most of the treasures of the ruins are there, in the Museo Nacional, where one can see them displayed under and behind glass, in protective isolation, no longer housed in their original buildings, no longer protecting the dead from annihilation.

Two hundred and seventy-five long miles, on a ribbon of a road from Uxmal to the campgrounds at Kailuum: We traveled through the endless henequen fields. Sometimes there were little oases of red water at the side of the road created by massive mangrove trees. We took many detours, driving very slowly through villages where the thatched-roofed palapa houses, the same structures that the ancient Mayans lived in at Chichén Itzá and Uxmal, surround a small cenote, the heart of the village. Only old women and young children were visible. One boy brought an armadillo to our car when we had to stop for a bump constructed across the road and indicated he wished to sell it. Another elderly lady in a spotless white embroidered dress held a similar one up for me to consider. The bumps serve their purpose of bringing cars to a stop; the vendors stand close to them. We smiled and replied in Spanish, and then remembered that the language here is Mayan. We did not know a word of it.

Further on we came upon fields of chicle, a crop that is important to the Mayan economy. It is transported north to chewing-gum factories, wrapped invitingly to be sold in supermarkets to occupy the constantly masticating mouths of millions of Americans. We saw the workers bringing blocks of the gummy substance to the side of the road. Most of them have 'chiclero's ear': parts of these organs have been eaten away by an insect that lives in the chicle fields and feeds on humans.

∽

Tired but exhilarated, we settled into a week of rest and mindless, sunlit, waterlogged relaxation at the campgrounds in Kailuum. Sybil arrived by air from Washington, and taxi from Cancún, having seen to all the house-selling chores. Everywhere at Kailuum there was evidence of the terrible devastation done by Hurricane Gilbert six months ago. The old palm trees along the beach and behind the campgrounds had been uprooted, beach sand transported to roads, and the dining room destroyed and then restored by hardworking Mayan residents who first rebuilt their own houses and then much of the camp.

But the tents were up, the primitive, comfortable furnishings in place, the two bathhouses restored, and the blue-green Caribbean, once again calm and unthreatening, still lay a few feet away. For seven days we slept, ate, walked barefoot in the sand that was everywhere, snorkeled, talked to new acquaintances, swam, lay in our hammocks, drank and ate again, and went to bed to read by candlelight, the camp lacking electricity.

We saw trails of pelicans cross the enormous blue sky. I remembered hearing of a woman swimming in the waters off Cozumel who was taken for a fish by a pelican and attacked, and had to have seven stitches in her scalp. These pelicans looked too set on their path towards Cancún to stop for a human head.

As I always do, I took note of what people were reading on the beach. A beach book is easily characterized. Its garish cover and sun-browned pages are curled, spotted, and swelled by salt water from the hands of its owner. It smells of suntan lotion, and is always thick, on the owners' widely held belief that a very long book serves the time better and is more sustaining than a thin one. It is usually by James Michener, Tom Tryon, Ken Follett, Louis L'Amour, Stephen King, or John le Carré, occasionally by Anne Tyler, John Irving, or Toni Morrison, never by Nathaniel Hawthorne, Herman Melville, or Charles Dickens, although these chaps also wrote absorbing stories of considerable length.

If one is reading on the beach, there is nothing to prevent constant interruptions by acquaintances walking by. Many people assume that reading is a poor substitute for *doing something,* not valuable in itself. My mother, as I remember, supported this view. Seeing me reading on the couch, she would say: 'If you're not doing anything, would you mind setting the table?'

Sybil remembers that a girl caught reading a book in her family was especially vulnerable. Spotted by her mother when Sybil was so engaged, she would invariably be asked to do a chore.

After several such interruptions, Sybil said, 'Why don't you ask Jim [her older brother who was also reading] to do it?'

Her mother: 'Because he's studying.'

One morning I put my wooden beach chair facing the sea under the single surviving palm tree near our tent, to read. It is the only possible orientation at Kailuum: One goes into and comes from it, looks at it endlessly, sits beside it, swims and wades in it, walks beside it, and watches the sun rise and, by reflection, go down over it. Half-buried in the sand I found an abandoned, thick paperback book, in a genre I don't especially enjoy: science fiction. I read a bit in it. It was about a young girl endowed with ESP who disrupts the life of what the author described as a middle-aged man. A few pages on, the man is further described as thirty-four years old. I reburied the book in the sand.

Another morning, unable to concentrate on the revisions I should have been making on *Camp,* I left my manuscript under my chair and went to talk to a young, bearded fellow who seemed to be surveying the beach. He told me he had been hired by the Mexican government to see what could be done to restore the hurricane-ravaged reefs and beaches. He said the reef off Kailuum had been badly damaged.

'But I can't get mad at the sea,' he said. 'What makes me furious is that the Mexican government is knowingly allowing

developers to threaten the whole shore, from Cancún almost as
far down as Tulum.'

He told me a long, horrifying story of coastal destruction in
Yucatán. He had advised the government about proper sewage
control provisions for a newly erected, very large resort south of
us, called Aventura. It is lavish, expensive, but carelessly planned
and built, with only minor inspection by local or provincial
officials. His advice went unheeded. So, in a few years, he
predicted, the land area and waters around the resort will be
polluted. I told him we had been able to smell the pollution in
the lagoon in Cancún as we drove along the stretch of more
than a hundred new, glossy hotels that clearly must be emptying
their sewage into it.

He said, sadly: "Oh yes, the sewage treatment plants are not
sufficient for the building that has taken place. The town of
Carmen del Playa is in the same danger. It is overpopulated and
straining the water and sewage services."

We stood together staring out at Kailuum's clean water and
immaculate beach.

'How long do you think this will stay this way?' I asked
him.

'Not long,' he said glumly. 'I've been told that the Mexican
government has sold a large strip of beachfront and acres of land
to the Hilton people, just five miles north of here. They may ask
me to do a study of the service needs for a hotel of hundreds of
rooms. I will do it, make recommendations, but inevitably
money will change hands, American money into official
Mexican hands, because Mexico is poor and needs the money.
Holes will be dug into rock for the refuse, so it will spread
sideways, and inevitably, someday pollute the water.'

'Terrible,' I said. He started down the beach carrying his
equipment, saying nothing more.

The last morning, dreading the thought of leaving, we were

up at five-thirty to watch the sun rise. I thought of Auden, who said once: 'Those who hate to go to bed fear death, those who hate to get up fear life.' What of those, like me, who can't wait to get up? Do we not fear the death that lying in bed represents?

Walking along the beach to our last breakfast at the camp, Sybil and I talked about our house in Washington, as if to prepare ourselves for being gone from here, and back there at the end of this day. Her eyes filled with tears. She said she clings to the house, reluctant to let it go, hating the prospect of change, wishing we didn't have to sell it, feeling it is our one place she thought she would always be secure. I wonder why *I* am not sad about leaving the house, only my studio in the carriage house.

We ate fruit and sweet buns and drank coffee in silence. I believe I knew what she was thinking (presumptuous, surely), and I regretted my own deep and perpetual selfishness. I mourn the passing of the carriage house because *that is where my work is.* I contemplate the end of our residence on North Carolina Avenue without regret because I have always felt an irrational need to break ties when they threaten to be permanent. It is not that I am confident of what life in Maine will be like—the prospect of fixing the house there to make it livable for us is frightening—but that, for a brief period, I will be gone from here and hardly settled there; and that seems to me to be a kind of odd freedom. Sybil has agreed that the first room to be redone in the Maine house will be my study. Once I am settled in it, I will be happy and at home, with my work, my books, my manuscripts, my computer, and the chattering, efficient printer.

Walking back to our tent to pack, I saw, at the edge of the clearing where all the destroyed trees are heaped, the roots of what I thought was a manzanita tree. I remember hearing from a native on St. John in the Virgin Islands that every part of this tree—roots, leaves, flowers, stems—is poisonous. Columbus called its fruit 'death apple.' To see it dead instead of flourishing made Kailuum's devastation by Gilbert a little less satanic.

On the plane, I talked to a businessman coming home from a conference in Cancún. Twice he rounded off anecdotes about his stay with the same favorite (these days) phrase: 'The bottom line is . . .' And once he answered a question with another popular formulation that I have grown tired of: 'There is good news and bad news. The good news is . . .' People seize upon these clichés as though they had just thought them up. They use them in place of simple or original rhetoric. I can only hope to live long enough to see such language swell up in volume, explode, die, and disappear.

The flight attendants on the plane had movable wagons that completely filled the aisle. Once they began to serve from them, drinks, and then food, and then drinks again, it was impossible to pass them, to go to the bathroom or, if one was foresighted and made it to the bathroom, to get back to one's seat. An unaccustomed claustrophobic panic welled up in me, caused, perhaps, by two weeks of wandering about in the expanses of ancient cities and living beside the endless sea. Now I was confined to a seat, strapped into it, with two people on one side and the barely mobile wagon on the other. I should have been gracious, I suppose, and accepted this state of affairs as instructive preparation for my return to the city and our narrow Victorian house, walled in by a hundred cartons of books and possessions.

෴

February 22: This morning I learn, through a *Washington Post* obituary, that Rudy von Abele has died. He was a colleague of mine at American University who retired a year or so before I did. He had taught for many years and was an enigmatic figure to me, brilliant, talented, almost a dwarf of a man, with very bad eyes and a great love for the work of Joyce, Yeats, and Beckett, German classical music, mystery stories, and young women. He had written one novel I admired, *The Party,* an equally good book of poems published by a university press, and a perceptive study of Nathaniel Hawthorne. Good students trusted and admired him, poor ones feared and misunderstood him.

I never knew him well. Indeed, I thought he rather disliked me. The last time I saw him was at the door to his apartment. I called to tell him I had received an extra copy of the new three-volume critical and synoptic edition of Joyce's *Ulysses,* and would be glad to give it to him. He said, yes, he would like to have it, and told me where he lived. Sybil and I drove to the apartment house on Massachusetts Avenue and rang his bell. He opened the door a crack.

'I've brought the *Ulysses,*' I said.

'Thank you,' he said, reached out, took the books, and closed the door. I never saw him again.

Strangely enough, after this curious dismissal, he told his executor to offer his books for sale to Wayward Books after his death. Sybil spoke to his executor today and arranged to pick up the key to the apartment next week and look at the books.

∽

Back in my study. It now begins to resemble a warehouse. The bookcases are bare, the once ample walking space is filled with cartons, pictures and memorabilia are gone from the walls. But packing up in the study is very slow because I keep finding books I have forgotten I had. Today I sat on a pile of cartons to read from a collection of essays by George Bernard Shaw and came upon a typically Shavian view of women. (He is thought by many eager enlisters in the cause to have been an early feminist.)

> No fascinating woman ever wants to emancipate her sex. Her object is to gather power into the hands of Man, because she knows she can govern him. She is no more jealous of his nominal supremacy than he himself is jealous of the strength and speed of his horse. Women disguise their strength as womanly weakness, their audacity as womanly timidity, their unscrupulousness as womanly innocence, their impunities as womanly defenselessness; simple men are duped by them, and subtle ones disarmed and intimidated. It is only the proud, straightforward women who wish, not to govern, but to be free. . . .

A finely shaped piece of rhetoric, saved from patriarchal condescension only by the last sentence.

∽

A letter today from Kay Boyle, who has moved back to the Bay Area, Oakland, to be near her son. She is a miraculous woman, a phoenix, rising up and surviving one almost mortal illness after another. I think of her often, remembering at odd moments in the day the wise things she has said or written to me over the twenty years I have known her. Whenever I start to write in this memoir about my troubles writing *Camp,* the painful rejection of *The Habit,* the strain of trying to remember accurately what I did, I recall her warning that 'the less writers write about their own work, the better.'

Her unselfish devotion to the well-being of others, to the commonweal, is her most notable characteristic. In her eighties she is still active in Amnesty International, and still is writing. She differs from a writer like Tillie Olsen, who wrote what she had to say in the thirties and has spent the next fifty years nursing her writer's block, caressing her early reputation, and rationalizing her sterility by blaming it on her hard life as a working woman. I remember Kay telling me she once had to write her novels at night in the bathroom perched on the toilet seat, after her six children were cared for and put to bed.

During the Vietnam War, Kay stood on the steps of the Federal Building in San Francisco (with Joan Baez's mother, her good friend) and burned the draft cards of the young men in the crowd. When she came down, she met Tillie, standing on the edge of the gathering, who said: 'Oh Kay, I so admire you for what you are doing. How I wish I were doing it.'

Kay's response: 'Why don't you, Tillie?'

∾

Writers' blocks are real and terrible afflictions. I know that. But at times they are the excuse for not wanting to finish the task at hand, or for the discovery that one has nothing more to say, or the result of having wasted the initial, vital energy that began the enterprise, with talk.

So it was with Katherine Anne Porter. Late in her life I went to have tea with her in her apartment in College Park, Maryland. She looked quite wonderful, her white hair beautifully coiffed, her neck decorated with her fine emeralds. I told her I wondered about the fate of her book on Cotton Mather. I had come upon an old catalogue issued by Horace Liveright which advertised a volume by her called *The Devil and Cotton Mather* to appear in the fall of 1927. It read: '. . . Miss Porter has given us an astounding picture of religious ecstasy and righteousness. . . . as a study of a pious and bigoted figure, this book . . . is an important document.'

Apparently all that Liveright had in hand when he issued his catalogue was a sketch for the book. He gave Katherine Anne Porter three hundred dollars to complete the research and

deliver the ms. Her biographer, Joan Givner, told me Porter had
done some research in Salem on the subject she had chosen,
under the mistaken notion that Mather was a witch-burner. She
was disappointed to find nothing to substantiate her belief. She
became aware of the vastness of the already well-documented
material; at the same time she discovered that what she had
preconceived to be a villainous character was not so. From
Bermuda she wrote to Liveright for more money, saying she
had by now read more than four hundred books for background
on the subject.

She did write three error-ridden chapters that she sent to the
publisher, and which appeared in print in small magazines in the
forties. Again the same notice of the book appeared in Boni &
Liveright's catalogue for 1928. But in 1929 the chapters stopped
coming to Liveright. He wrote. She replied four months later,
asking him to stop announcing the book. She could not finish it,
she said, because of the demands of other work.

In 1934, Robert MacAlmon (Kay Boyle's beloved friend)
wrote that Porter was secluded in Paris writing a biography of
Cotton Mather. That was the last she was heard from on the
subject.

Her reply to my question was angry. She no longer smiled in
her wide Southern-belle way. 'The past is past,' she said, 'and
I'm glad of it. Half of my work is still undone. Actually I've
written *ten* chapters of that book. I've given up trying to do it,
until all the rest of it can be done at once. I had to stop because
the Sacco-Vanzetti case came up and I needed to be active in
that.

'But no one realizes, when they talk of my not doing this or
finishing that, that I always had to earn a living as a writer,
speaking, journalism, teaching. I wasn't *free* to finish the book.
Sometime I will, of course.'

I believe the truth is that she ran out of interest in the

subject, very early in the research. Givner agrees, saying she never wanted to write about anything if she could not shape the facts to her way of thinking. All the rest, the excuses, the fifty-year delay, the good intentions, are what a writer uses when the truth is not suitable.

Some writers are encouraged by advances and race on to finish the book. But there are those for whom it is fatal to discuss a work-in-progress or to accept an advance before it is finished. Like my father, for whom promises were always a more than adequate substitute for fulfillment of them.

∽

Over here in the carriage house, alone with my packed possessions and covered, silent computer, I see the light go on in the kitchen in the house, and know that Sybil is home and beginning to fix dinner. I realize I have been here since seven-thirty in the morning and it is now seven-thirty again, time to go through the list of things I must check before I leave this peaceful den. And at the end, a new entry, caused by the visual requirements of the computer's monitor: Change glasses.

What I need to remember is to go through the list carefully, or else I may well burn down this overelectrified little house before I have a chance to move out of it. I do this, nod goodbye to the space I love, go downstairs and across the garden, abandoning my twelve hours of silence. In an old notebook that I put into the box for the University of Virginia this morning I found a sentence by Rainer Maria Rilke: 'Love consists in this: that two solitudes protect and touch, and greet each other.'

I climb the stairs to the deck, open the kitchen door, and greet Sybil.

All evening we pack books from the dining-room walls. I find a volume I haven't looked at in fifty years, a thin, blue-cloth-covered little book entitled *Notes on a Half Century of*

United States Naval Ordnance. One of my commanding officers, Captain Wilbur R. Van Auken, handed it to me when I left his station in Washington, D.C., to go to the Twelfth Naval District in San Francisco. It is warmly inscribed, with the identifying letters 'WAVES, USNR' after my name, and the date, June 1944. Beyond that, I have no memory of him at all. Tonight I tried to read it and found I was able to get only as far as most of the first sentence of his book: 'This year 1880 in ordnance, under Commodore Jeffers, is selected as it marks the beginning of the manufacture of the first hooped steel, high-powered rifled guns . . .' I decided to pack the book for the tie to the past it represented. Then I sat down to rest and thought about another commanding officer I reported to after my assignment to the Bureau of Ordnance in Washington.

He too was a captain, retired, and called back to serve in a noncombatant role in the Navy. I cannot remember his name, but I can see his face clearly: fat, puffy, ruddy, a nose that was stippled, suggesting long, heavy drinking. I never saw him smile. I think he must have resented his relatively inactive job and most of all the number of commissioned women (women! In the United States Navy!) under his command.

Our station was in an office building on New Montgomery Street in San Francisco. The day I reported for duty, spic and span in a freshly pressed uniform, my transfer papers stowed in a neat blue folder, was bright and shining with the yellow light I have only seen in that beautiful city on its seven hills. I took the elevator to the sixth floor, taking off my warm hat and gloves, hating to come in out of the lovely day. I was directed to the cubicle of the 'officer of the deck.' His title, solemnly engraved over his door, was my first hint of the nature of things to come. The *deck?*

He was a straight-faced, thin, young lieutenant senior grade. He told me to sit down, and then informed me of the rules of the station and the ritual I was to follow when I reported to the captain. He said the captain called the sixth floor of the office building the 'ship.'

Sighing, I set off to find the captain's quarters. As I had been instructed, I put on my shining new officer's hat and white gloves and knocked once on the captain's door.

'Enter,' he said.

Standing as erect as I could, I approached his desk and put my papers down in the in-box as I had been told to do. I saluted and said:

'Ensign Grumbach reporting for duty, sir.'

The captain stood up, put on his hat with its assemblage of gold braid on the visor, and said:

'Welcome aboard, ensign.'

And I, as instructed, replied:

'Glad to be aboard, sir.'

This was to be a year of absurd naval etiquette. The captain was not to be denied his right to command a ship even on New Montgomery Street. Before every shift we served we rode the elevator to the sixth floor, took two steps out of the cage, turned slightly toward the large American flag mounted on a platform down the hall, and saluted the poop deck at the stern of the ship. If the officer of the deck was anywhere around, we were required to ask permission to come aboard, sir.

If a goodly number of naval personnel were aboard the elevator, it would take a little time to complete this operation before the elevator, carrying irritated civilians on their way to their jobs on the upper floors, could be emptied. But respect to the poop deck was not to be denied our captain.

Regularly, we had white-glove inspections, to see that our desks and cubicles were shipshape. Sometimes the captain, in full uniform, held an unannounced tour of inspection. He ran his finger over the tops of our Royal typewriters to assure himself they were not gathering dust. On occasion, bells would ring throughout the floor, and we would line up before the elevator doors. This was termed, seriously, 'abandon ship drill.' We would ride down to the lobby and stand around in congenial little groups to await the call to come aboard again. So it went.

I remember that, near the end of my time there, the captain seemed to feel that the rules of the Navy were not reaching far enough. The order went out that the block on which the building stood, and the street across from it, were now constituted decks of the ship. On those streets enlisted men were to salute officers, and officers were to return the salute. Now you must know that in those years, San Francisco was a Navy town, with naval personnel of every rank and rate cramming its streets. To salute every officer one passed, especially *women* officers, was an absurdity to the hundreds of enlisted men and women on our street. So they would step down into the gutter and walk along the edge of the traffic to avoid saluting on the sidewalk. They were on the water, they claimed, and gutter travel came to be known as the Jesus walk.

On second thought, I removed the little book on naval ordnance from the packing carton and put it into one marked 'Giveaway.'

ॐ

For review, the letters of Stephen Crane arrived today. Last week I browsed through a volume of Henry James's letters to Edmund Gosse. Crane's letters are very fragmentary, very few of them of any real consequence. James's to Gosse are extremely short, and many of them dwell on appointments they had with each other, or their illnesses.

In the great rush to publish every word put down by respected writers of the past and the present, too often we are given books of largely worthless letters, collections of stray papers that should have been destroyed by the author, journals not intended to reach any reader's eyes. Juvenilia better left to the trash sometimes is published as an 'important' volume of 'discoveries' or 'significant' work of an earlier period.

But I started to talk about the letters of Crane and James/Gosse. I am comforted to see that occasionally these letters resemble my own in quality, significance, content. So often I write to a friend, then read over the empty prose and wish I had striven for more elegant, memorable expression. Now I feel relieved that I have precedents for my ordinariness and quotidian subject matter. I can only hope no recipient is saving them with the intention of committing them to print.

∽

Two items from a 1977 notebook in the pile awaiting pickup by the librarian of the University of Virginia:
  • Piece of a Louise Bogan poem called 'Women':

> Women have no wilderness in them,
> They are provident instead,
> Content in the tight hot cell of their hearts
> To eat dusty bread.

'No wilderness in them.' Reminiscent of Joyce's admonition to the young would-be novelist who, Joyce thought, did not have enough chaos in him to be a writer.
  • Visiting a friend, Edward Kessler, on Clark's Island off the coast of Duxbury in Massachusetts. Ed tells me about the island's oldest inhabitant. Every year on her birthday, now well into her nineties, very arthritic, and walking with two canes, she climbs painfully into her boat and rows twice around the island.

∽

Out of the same notebook falls an almost transparent piece of paper which, at first, I cannot identify. I spread out the three square sheets, which are connected to each other by perforations, and read at the bottom of each in pale-blue ink: GOVERNMENT PROPERTY. Then I remember. The paper comes from rolls serving the toilets in the bathroom of the British Museum. I remember being delighted to find, when I was working on the Mary McCarthy biography years ago in the lovely reading room of that library, that every sheet of toilet paper in public buildings was similarly inscribed.

∽

Sybil and I continue to disagree about what should go to Maine, what should remain in Washington in the apartment we have taken on the Hill to afford us a retreat in the cold months in Maine, and what should be sent to storage. I want everything I value to go to the new house, she wants much of what she cares about to stay here in the apartment. We are divided by what we most cherish and where we most wish to be. It may work out: I may lose my preference for the isolated life by the sea and want to return to the city, she may wear out her long-held ties to crowds, theaters, and her bustling bookshop, and settle for the quiet life beside the cove. If we are still at odds, we will have to find a middle ground on which to combine our passions.

Her requirements always seem unimportant to me, and mine, I'm sure, to her. I worry that she will perceive how selfish my motives are for where I wish to be. I remember Ford Madox Ford writing in *The Good Soldier:* 'For it is intolerable to live constantly with one human being who perceives one's small meannesses.'

༄

Sybil and I go to Rudy von Abele's apartment to see his books.
We are alone among his possessions: some pictures, bookcases, a
few pieces of furniture, compact disks, records, and a large
collection of books. The dust that lies over everything suggests
the particles of his person, as well as the manner of his bachelor
existence. This was a man who loved and taught the great
modern Irish writers. We look eagerly at the volumes of early
Joyce and Beckett and find first editions among them. But they
turn out to be working copies of the books, full of heavy
marginal notes and incomprehensible numbers, much of his
notation in ink. An interesting scholar's library, but
unfortunately not many volumes salable as pristine first editions.

I am intrigued by the 125 compact disks of Bach, Beethoven,
Brahms, Mozart, and a few moderns like Stravinsky. When
Sybil makes an offer for most of Rudy's books—first editions or
not, they are interesting, useful books for a general
bookstore—I ask the executor if I could buy the disks. Now,
ready to hand, in one swoop, I have another collection of music
which, in its technology, supersedes all my old records and
newer cassettes. I suppose the day will come when all recorded
music will be reduced to tiny thimbles of superb quality, and
these extraordinary disks will be outmoded. Now our old
record player stands idle, the cassette player will be used only
occasionally, and the new compact disk player, which Sybil
bought as her share of the disk expense, will serve us. All this
change in less than thirty years, after generations of the beloved
Victrola, for which I remember sharpening reed needles. My
big, black, shining, breakable 78s, badly scratched and
inaccurate, are now collectors' items, beloved to me as old
furniture and ancestral tintypes, but not very valuable for
listening pleasure.

∽

Sybil is away for the end of the week, doing a book fair. I am here alone in this almost-packed-up house, enjoying the solitude. Packing a volume of Susan Sontag, I impede my progress, as usual, by stopping to read. She quotes Cesare Pavese on love: 'What one takes to be an attachment to another person, is unmasked as one more dance of the solitary ego.' So it is, I think, true at least in part. In modern cliché, the buck stops at the egocentric self, even when it appears to be love of the other.

∽

Sybil comes home; I am glad to have my solitude ended. We go to see an exhibit of David Smith sculpture. Next to me, two matronly ladies discuss a black, linear, wrought-iron horse and buggy.

One: 'Now, what do you think about that?'

Long pause. Then, the other: 'Well, a lot of work must have gone into it.'

∽

Sign in front of a Presbyterian church on Capitol Hill: CHURCH-GOING FAMILIES ARE HAPPIER. How can the pastor know? Would it were always so.

∽

I buy a loaf of rye bread from the bakery in the Eastern Market. I cut a piece and find the bread is stale. I remember Harry Grumbach, my father-in-law, telling me that in *real* Jewish bakeries, the lady who sells the bread digs her long fingernail into the crust to prove its freshness.

March

*K*ey West: I speak at a seminar on the short story, with John Edgar Wideman and Jane Smiley. We are put up in an opulent hotel that looks out on the Gulf. My suite has a sauna, two enormous rooms, a fully equipped kitchen, and sweeping balconies. For what I have to say on the subject, the housing seems excessive. The first morning, after breakfast, I take a walk to the pool area (there does not seem to be a beach) and come upon two very old, fat women who are identical twins. They walk arm in arm, matching their tiny steps, their sausage arms embracing each other behind their backs. Both wear bright new Nike sneakers, powder-blue raincoats tightly belted about their middles (they have no waists), the same top button undone under each flabby throat, and light polyester slacks stretched over their heavy legs. They appear to be outlandish caricatures, female Tweedledee and Tweedledum, almost obscene human figures. I wonder: Why do they dress alike? Because all their lives they have? Because they like the attention identical twins receive? Because they love themselves in each other, even in their present weighty state?

∽

I take a small motorboat out to a reef to snorkel, on the advice
of a Key Westerner at the conference. The boat is very old and
shakes curiously. I distract myself from what appears to me to be
the threat of the boat's flying apart at any moment by trying to
remember the word I learned recently (the British use it
frequently) for vibrating violently: to judder. By the time my
personal computer has retrieved the word, the boat arrives, still
juddering, at the reef. The reef is disappointing, lacking both
fish and interesting coral.

∽

There is no escape from the terrible realities of this decade, even
down here in this land of somehow artificial sunshine,
green-water pools, and warmth that feels like steam heat. A
memorial service is held for an old friend, Jim Boatwright, a
winter resident of Key West and editor of the noted quarterly
Shenandoah. Those of us at the conference who knew him leave
the official doings and go to a small house on a side street.
There, in his garden, poets and novelists, editors and friends
listen to writers—Peter Taylor, Richard Wilbur, James
Merrill—read from the poetry that Boatwright loved.
I remember his bright, handsome, lively, sunburned
face because later, when we go through his house and into the
garden on the other side for wine and cheese, we are offered a
keepsake, a recent picture of him. He is still smiling in
this last photograph, but his face is sunken, his eyes deeply
ringed. He has been ravaged by the unforgivable scourge,
AIDS.

I weep through the whole reading, for Jim, and Bill, and
Robert, and Michael, and Tom Victor, and Richard, and
thousands of others who have gone with them.

∾

Henry Miller: 'For the person who feels, life's a tragedy. For the person who thinks, it's a comedy.' Clearly I have never thought enough.

∾

The service, or perhaps the food or water in the lavish hotel, have upset my stomach. On my way on foot to see the Ernest Hemingway House, I go into a restaurant with an outside café to ask to use the bathroom. The hostess seems reluctant, explaining that too many people come in for just that purpose. I must have looked desperate, because she finally agrees, and says:
    'Don't mind the sink.'
    The sink is not the object of my interest. But when I finish with the toilet, I turn to it to wash. Coiled in the bowl is a realistic green plastic snake, intended, I suppose, to discourage further use of the facility, a new variety of Southern hospitality.

∾

I sit on the balcony and watch the sun go down over the Gulf. Crowds are lined up on the wharf. As the last cusp of sun disappears into the now-yellow sea, everyone down there bursts into applause. Later I learn this is a local custom. People come to the edge of the water on sunny evenings to clap for the sunset.
    Seated there as the light dies, I think of an idea for a story. A woman (professional of some sort) is about to be married for the second time, entirely certain that this approaching alliance with a cultivated, sophisticated, mature man will avoid all the mad excitement, violent sexual encounters, and, ultimately, severe disappointments of her first marriage. They decide to spend the two weeks before the ceremony apart, he visiting his elderly

parents, she in Yucatán. In Mérida she meets a young, handsome Mayan named Luis (?) who carries her baggage from her rented car to the hotel. He suggests he come back to her room that evening. Surprising herself, she agrees. Their lovemaking is passionate, even violent, unbelievably enjoyable. She realizes Luis is very much like her first husband. Will she marry again?

∽

Heard in the street in Key West: 'Give me a ring up sometime.'
  'Listen up.'
  'Looky here.'
  'Did you make out with him?'
  'I took it offen him.'
  The reply by one lady to everything said by her companion: 'Isn't it something?'

∽

Beside the pool between swims I am reading a new first novel by a very young woman whose story is anguished, self-pitying, revealing the disturbed state of her mind. I remember Simone de Beauvoir writing: 'In one way or another, every book is a cry for help.' This one is filled with raw, undigested teenage experience. I think of T. S. Eliot's lines: '. . . the end of all our exploring/Will be to arrive where we started/And know the place for the first time.' This young novelist has not given herself time for the creative chaos, the wildness, to collect and simmer. She needs to leave the scene of her first experience, take journeys in every direction, return, and then explore the truths of the place she started from.

   George Eliot wrote her first novel *(Adam Bede)* when she was forty.

∽

On the plane home from Key West I sit beside a lady who tells me she makes her living as a house painter and wallpaper hanger. I tell her I always thought hanging wallpaper one of the most difficult tasks in the world. She agrees. 'It is a terrible strain. Especially after I paper bathrooms. For weeks afterwards, every time the phone rings, I think it is an angry customer to say the paper is coming off the wall.'

ᔭ

Washington. Spring comes early here. It is late March, and yet crocuses are up around our elm tree in the front yard, the trees everywhere are in light-green bud, and the air is promising warmth. Even the sun has taken on a new brightness, coloring the customary grey Washington air so that it now looks yellower.

Today I tape five book reviews at National Public Radio, trying to avoid my usual stammering, sibilants and misreadings. But my new producer is a nervous man, a chain smoker, restless, never motionless. I catch his jitters, and read badly. I wish I had studied speech in college. I remember that in grade school the wealthier students used to take 'elocution lessons.'

One of the books I reviewed was by Brenda Ueland, who died, after 'an active and vital life' (as the blurb to her book on writing says), in 1985 at the age of ninety-three. 'Vital life' seems rather redundant.

Her book, written fifty years ago, is called *If You Want to Write* and subtitled 'A Book About Art, Independence and Spirit.' It is full of eccentric, unexpected, unusual, freewheeling advice, always encouraging the ambitious, apprentice young writer to:

'Write freely, recklessly, in first drafts.'

'Try to discover your true, honest, untheoretical self.'

'When discouraged, remember what Van Gogh said: "If you

hear a voice within you saying, You are no painter, then paint by all means, lad, and that voice will be silenced, but only by working." '

About fifteen years ago I made friends with Brenda Ueland. She had written to me at *The New Republic* to cancel her long-held subscription ('Since the forties,' she wrote) because she was low in funds, and because she thought the writing ('mostly by men, I notice') was often too 'fancy.'

I replied, asking her to accept a complimentary subscription, and promising to watch out for the quality of the writing, at least in the back of the book, which I edited. A letter came back at once from her (she lived in Minneapolis). It contained a check and an apology. 'I've decided, feeling shamed, that I *can* afford it.'

From then on we wrote to each other on occasion. Her letters contained long, detailed advice on how to eat more healthily (bran, no refined sugar or white flour, no caffeine or alcohol), and accounts of her exercise program, which included a yearly climb up Pikes Peak in her seventies, running, swimming, and walking: her suggestion was that I 'walk a thousand miles this year . . . [it is] hardly three miles a day.'

When I left *The New Republic* and began to consider writing about Willa Cather, I came upon Ueland's autobiography, called *Me,* published in 1939. I learned that she had known Edith Lewis, Cather's companion for forty years. 'She [Lewis] was my boss at *Every Week,* Bruce Barton's magazine,' she wrote. Every now and then, Ueland said, she would be invited to dinner at 5 Bank Street, where Cather and Lewis lived in 'a long, railroad apartment.' She said the food cooked by their French cook, Josephine, was excellent.

In *Me,* Ueland had written that Cather was 'masculinely intellectual.' What did she mean, exactly? I asked. She responded: 'Solid, thoughtful, learned, spoke in complete and excellent sentences. . . . Splendid, grave, vigorous . . . compact, not at all flabby or abdominal but there was no concave waistline. . . . Bright red cheeks and bright green eyes. A good nose. Strong teeth. . . . Not chic, not masculine, but handsome, strong. She might have been a Marchioness.'

Of Edith Lewis she wrote that she was in awe of so perfect a boss who 'was also a woman.' I recognized her slight misogyny.

I asked her if she had any notion of the nature of their relationship. She responded indignantly: 'No. We had not the slightest tincture of a notion about that. Such a thought—a horrible libel and affront to their grandeur, nobility, sense of beauty, seemliness, grace.' She ended a long paragraph of indignation with a somewhat modified if muddled view:

'I am ninety years old and have had a wonderful, impassioned life, but I am far too polite, too respectful of all others to let myself *imagine* other people's copulations. I censure it out. All love is interesting and worthy of our sympathy.'

Ueland was a remarkable woman. Robert Penn Warren was her friend, she was invited by Warren Beatty to be in his movie *Reds,* because she had known John Reed well, she was responsible for getting Harry Reasoner his first newspaper job. She was knighted by the King of Norway, and, in her eighties, set a swimming record. Just before she died, she was still walking three miles, and attending to her large correspondence. Fifty years after it first appeared, she provided a new introduction to the second edition of her book on writing.

༄

A good comment from an editor on *Camp,* accompanied by the regret that it is too slight to launch a whole publishing program with. I begin to wonder if the novella has any value at all. I feel I am playing a partner in that game I Doubt It, which I used to play with my sister, who is a character in *Camp.*

Do not despair, I tell myself. Years ago at Yaddo, Alice
Walker sat down beside me at dinner and said: 'I'm working on
a novel, but something is missing and I don't know what it is.' I
think it turned out to be *The Color Purple*.

༄

Lunch, on the deck in a warm mid-March noon. I hear a tapping
noise. The boy next door with his ball? Someone typing (or
tap-dancing) across the alley? No. I see it now. A woodpecker at
work on our elm tree.

I take my tray back into the kitchen and remember the sign
someone once tacked up over the pantry at the MacDowell
Colony: 'It is not enough to have talent. You also have to carry
in your dishes.'

༄

'You have a certain panache,' an old acquaintance said to me
yesterday. I wonder what he meant. I have a vision of myself
wearing a great Mayan headdress, since the Latin means feathers
or tassels, and I always thought 'panache' meant an ornamental
plume of feathers.

༄

Last Sunday in March. At the coffee hour in St. James Church, a
few of us meet to talk about joining an AIDS aid group to
work in Capitol Hill Hospital. The organization, throughout
the diocese, already has its own acronym (no group in this
capital city survives without one): ECRA, Episcopal Caring
Response to AIDS, an awkward formulation, I thought.

One of the participants is a handsome young military officer
in civilian clothes. He is a cheerful, spirited fellow full of jokes
and good stories. He tells me about his small nephew who
watched *Quo Vadis* on television and saw the Romans throw

what were called Christians to the lions in the Circus.

'Whew,' he said, 'I'm sure glad I'm a Catholic.'

A friend of his was told that the only requirement for his choice of a sponsor at his adult baptism was that the person be a good Christian. His reply: 'Are you trying to make this difficult for me?'

After the organizational meeting, the major in mufti had another narrative. Seems that Bismarck made very good use of his professed Christianity. During the Siege of Paris in 1871 he instructed his soldiers to shoot any civilian who asked for more food. He added: 'I attach no great importance to human life because I believe in another world.'

ᔕ

The *Washington Post* reports a high degree of semiliteracy in Washington high schools. Not too different from the state of things everywhere in the country, I think. A sentence is quoted from a student's essay: 'No man can no all there is to no of life.'

ᔕ

Packing. I stop to read in a volume of Gertrude Stein's. I find, as always in her work, sentences that take me aback, especially as I contemplate my own notebooks: 'Remarks are not literature.'

ᔕ

A CENTURY OF PROGRESS the banner across the entrance to one of the Smithsonian buildings reads. Progress: an illusion that persons living only in the present, ignorant of history, possess. To keep the world of Maya fresh in my mind, I have been rereading one of my favorite books. Victor Wolfgang von Hagen, in the introduction to a new edition of John Lloyd Stephens's *Incidents of Travel in Yucatán,* writes about Stephens and his illustrator Charles Catherwood. In 1848 they believed in

Manifest Destiny. 'They didn't know,' writes von Hagen, 'as we do now, that progress is neither automatic, universal, nor inevitable.'

∽

On the deck this afternoon I sit in a wedge of sun to read. A small bird (is it young?) crisscrosses rapidly from telephone wire to the elm tree, and back again. A small, restless, unsettled bird, feeling insecure about the anachronistic heat of the day I wonder: As it ages, will it slow down? When it reaches its equivalent of my age, will its wings flap more slowly? Will it have trouble remaining in the air, dipping, falling a little, rising again tiredly, coming down to drink from the petals of the impatiens, eating less having lost its appetite, resting on the deck rail, waiting for a renewal of energy? Has anyone ever seen an aging bird?

For that matter, I have never seen a baby pigeon or a baby sea gull. All members of those species seem about the same size. So perhaps I will never see a shrinking, old bird, losing its powers, declining into old age. How lucky for the species, how heartening to me.

∽

Sybil brings home some good, old books she has bought for the store. We sit in our chairs in the dining room. I watch her inspect each book minutely, its binding, the order and state of the illustrations and pages, the sewing of the signatures. Sometimes she sniffs it for mold. In each one, she reads a little, sometimes aloud to me, remarking on the good places. Often I take notes: Who knows when those words might 'come in useful,' as my mother used to say.

When the minute physical inspection and rapid scanning of the contents are finished, she puts a tentative price carefully on the right-hand corner of the flyleaf, and her secret code which tells her what she paid for the book. In the short time it has been in her hands, the book is hers, an orphan rescued from abandonment in someone's attic or cellar. Briefly she is its foster parent, giving it temporary shelter and solicitous attention. It is one of the lucky ones with another chance at life.

The life history of a new book is more often tragic than triumphant. Fresh from the press, offset or hand, it arrives at the bookseller's shelf full of hope. It has the unique, clean smell of optimism. In its sparkling, inviting, crisp jacket it appears to be smiling at the world, like a puppy in a pet-store window: 'Take me home.'

A few, fortunate best-sellers, well-reviewed books, books by respected or well-loved authors, are bought up at once and leave the shelves in a little flurry of triumph, like fortunate orphans chosen from asylum ranks for adoption who are leaving their less fortunate peers behind. The 'remainders,' as they will now be called, have lived out their shelf life, and are taken from their places of display after a few short weeks to be shipped back to their publishers. The publishers promptly turn them over to jobbers, businessmen who will deal with the crestfallen, disappointed volumes in bulk, offering them, at much lower prices, to retail booksellers and buyers looking for a bargain.

Off the books go again, now displayed on the bargain tables in chain bookstores. Those not purchased at their new half-price will be reduced, and then reduced again, until they all disappear. Where? Into homes where they are read, or simply fill shelves, or are displayed on a table, or lent, or stored and eventually sold when the owner needs more space or moves on or dies, to secondhand-book dealers.

Then the sad descent into oblivion begins. A few will be purchased. The rest will inhabit a used-book store for years in one dusty pile or another. At some point, the author and his work completely forgotten, the dealer despairs and puts them out in front of his store, marked ten cents each. Some might be bought by impecunious students, and the rest? After midnight, on a windy March night, a stinging rainstorm comes up, the books left out under a short canopy ('all you can fit into a paper bag') are soaked through, tossed into a garbage bin and hauled away to what in Maine is called, euphemistically, a 'transfer station.' So a saga of great hopes, ambition, even talent, disappears, under the obliterating grey ash of the town dump.

∽

Thursday I flew to Fort Lauderdale for a weekend gathering at the Broward Public Library. Before the plane could depart from Washington National Airport, it sat, fully loaded with passengers, in its landing dock for two hours so that repairs could be made to the hydraulic system. At last we advanced to the runway to find we were fourteenth in line for takeoff. Another stationary hour waiting our turn to fly. Then four hours to Florida. So, for seven hours, 150 people were cribbed and cabined together, occupying their time in a variety of ways.

Most of the passengers were college students, and four-fifths of them were female. Of course, I realized suddenly, it was spring break and they were on their way to a rollicking, alcoholic, sexually active life on the beach and in the sun. At first there were some loud, plaintive discussions about who would sit with whom and much seat-changing and baggage relocation from the overhead bins. This meant that mammoth purses the size of small valises (does anyone use this word now?) were lifted over and across me, since I had chosen to sit on the aisle. One, the heavy leather variety, grazed my head.

'Sorry,' the girl said, smiling broadly as she climbed over my legs. She seemed to have far more hair than head, and her lipstick had slipped, providing her with two pairs of lips.

My knees felt sore from her rough passing. I got into the
aisle to allow two substitutes into the vacated seats beside me.
They settled in quickly. The girl in the window seat put pink
foam earphones in place, closed her eyes to the magnificent array
of sunlit clouds, and immediately seemed to fall asleep. The girl
beside me had brought with her a paper cup of water. Holding
it carefully in one hand, she rummaged around in her large
handbag and pulled out a nail kit, put down the tray table in
front of her, spread out an assortment of implements beside the
cup of water, and began to 'do' her nails. Strong alcoholic odors
filled the air, causing people to stare over at her, making me feel
sleepy.

After a while I wished the polish remover had completely
anesthetized me. Talk between the manicurist and a girl in front
of her, who kneeled on her seat to watch the delicate
procedures, was excruciating. Boys (whom they called 'the
men') were the central, recurring subjects. The names and
descriptions of complicated beverages figured prominently in
the narratives about how they had spent the evening before. The
kneeler gave a graphic description of her date with Josh, who
vomited in the car after six glasses of rye. Elaborate plans and
locations of possible sites for encounters with beach men were
formulated. My seatmate expressed a liking for 'hunks'; the
kneeler preferred brains in men and could not understand why
she had even agreed to go out with Josh.

The conversation turned to Julie, a mutual friend at college,
who might be pregnant. She had gone home before midterms to
get money from her parents, just in case. . . . The word abortion
was never spoken. There were heated expressions of doubt about
the value of courses they were taking, the ability of their
professors to teach, and their own chances of passing one course
or another. The girl beside me, now blowing on her red-tipped
outstretched fingers, recalled her date last weekend with Lyman,

whose parents had it *all,* including a Jacuzzi, a hot tub, a heated swimming pool, two Mercedeses.

'*Awesome,*' said the apparently envious kneeler. She was quickly reassured by her friend that, on the other hand, Lyman was a complete weirdo, and very, very tight about money.

The plane bounced. Word came to fasten seat belts. The kneeler turned around and sat down.

The next hours were instructive. The covey of young women around me spent their time oddly (to my old-fashioned view). Not one of them opened a book or magazine or newspaper. Part of the time, when they were not conversing, their eyes seemed set unmoving in their heads, their expressions blank. They examined their nails, carefully, one by one, as though each were a miniature masterpiece. They conducted detailed searches into their voluminous purses. If their eyes were often inert, their hands were not. When not under inspection their fingers were engaged in playing with strands of their hair, twisting them into loose curls, then letting go and permitting the hair to return to its original Medusa shape.

Twice or three times an hour one of them would inspect her face in a pocket mirror retrieved from her purse-warren after much rummaging, find something wanting, throw the strap of her purse over her shoulder, and make for the lavatory at the back of the cabin. Twice I was struck in the face by the swinging containers as the young woman beside me went into the aisle. In the course of four hours in the air, she made a total of three such journeys.

When she returned, her face sparkled with fresh makeup. She settled down, stowed her purse, and began another session of staring ahead or falling asleep. Once again I opened my paperback, Marjorie Perloff's study of the poet Frank O'Hara, which I had been deterred from reading by my fascination with the theater going on around me. It was a little like living briefly

in Schubert Alley. But I didn't read at once, absorbed as I was
by the spectacle of these young women's contented emptiness. In
perfecting their persons, their eyes now shut, are they preparing
for the days ahead? Do they anticipate themselves stretched out
on the sunny beach on colorful towels, glistening with oil, their
eyes covered with dark glasses against the glare, turning every so
often in order to acquire an even tan, their minds once again
drained of thought?

I felt a sudden stroke of guilt at my excess of critical
scrutiny. Why should I have used all this time, better spent
reading Perloff on Frank O'Hara, taking mental notes, all
negative, on my fellow travelers? O'Hara wrote an early poem
about the critics of his poetry that Perloff uses as epigraph to her
book:

> I cannot possibly think of you
> other than you are: the assassin
>
> of my orchards. You lurk there
> in the shadows, meting out
>
> conversation like Eve's first
> confusion between penises and
>
> snakes. Oh be droll, be jolly
> and be temperate! Do not
>
> frighten me more than you
> have to! I must live forever.

Be temperate, I reminded myself. I have never been. I kept
inspecting them, like someone worrying a scab. They were all
dressed in what might be called a uniform: blue jeans,
T-shirts, sweat shirts emblazoned with pictures or sayings,
heavy socks and sneakers. They resembled gymnasts after a
hard workout, except for the pristine state of their faces and
hands, the contrived excesses of their hair.

How the requirements of dress have changed. I think of my father-in-law, who would never enter a restaurant, no matter how far he had traveled by car or how seedy the place looked, without wearing his starched white shirt and collar, tie, suit jacket, and fedora. No matter how inappropriate it might have seemed to others in the roadside fast-food place, he insisted on his lifelong outfit. He would inspect with distaste those around him, and remark in audible tones:

'Look at all those men. In their shirt sleeves. No tie. Where do they think they are? In the kitchen?'

Leonard, my former husband, inherited his father's fastidiousness. For years he wore black socks and wing-tipped shoes, shirt and tie, on Moody Beach, where we spent our summers. Only after a number of vacations in Maine did he ease into sneakers and sports shirts. But I often thought he never felt quite comfortable so attired. He had been equally strict about dress during World War II. I remember he never ventured twenty feet from our front door to the mailbox on the road without wearing his full uniform and fatigue cap.

Looking at the young women around me, I decided Leonard and Harry were anachronisms, old-fashioned, but insistently decorous and *proper*. I suppose to others they may have seemed absurd, much as the young women on the plane now appear to me, dressed for continental travel as though they were outfitted for a gymnasium or a softball game.

∽

Jane Emerson calls to report on Aunt Bet's health. She is Elizabeth Luther, Bob's great-aunt, who was 101 years old last October. Now she lives in a Northampton nursing home, alert, still quite beautiful and careful of her appearance (she has her hair and nails done regularly), confined to a wheelchair, but a constant reader when her eyes are up to it. She is about to have a

cataract operation to improve her ability to read. She loves
visitors, is a devoted smoker of cigarettes, and an imbiber of
apricot brandy to help her sleep.

At the celebration of her century birthday, people came
from all over New England to wish her well. President Ronald
Reagan (as he probably did to all centenarians) wrote to her.
Someone on television congratulated her. She recognized all her
visitors, and made them feel honored to be present at her party. I
could not be there, but I had a broadside made by a fine
letterpress printer in Oakland, California. It read:

AGE

There are so few who can grow old with grace, observed Richard
Steele in the *Spectator.* Elizabeth Blanchfield Luther is one of
the happy few.

How does one grow old with grace? There is a
prescription, I believe, but it is not easy to follow. We must
feel at home in the world, and then reside in peace with
ourselves. We must not so much demand to be loved as to
love. For if we love, selflessly and unpossessively, we are
then loved.

Note in the prescription that growing old with grace
must mean that somehow our resentments, selfishness,
ambitions, and grudges diminish. Compassion,
understanding, sympathy take their place. We sleep in
peace, we wake with pleasure to enjoy the music, poetry,
and glory of the natural world, rather than to rail against its
noise and threat, its clangor and crudeness, its misery,
meanness, and discord. We sense the spiritual in our
friends. We suspect God is in them, and in us.

Growing old gracefully is surrendering vanity and the
strident will, for the heart. As the Greek proverb says, *The
heart that loves is always young.*

The best part of the prescription is not an observation or

an order but a question posed by the immortal pitcher
Satchel Paige: *How old would you be if you didn't know how old
you was?*

I don't wish to idealize Aunt Bet. Asked about birthdays, she
says she wants no more of them, that she is tired of living. Yet
her behavior belies her pessimism. She *acts* as though living still
holds some pleasures for her. I believe she will come through
her eye surgery well. I am starting to collect new biographies
(which she most enjoys) to send her when it is over, not foolish
ones about movie or rock stars or political figures who have
committed crimes against the state or nation and then found
God in prison, but good, recent ones, of Willa Cather (by James
Woodress), of Ernest Hemingway (by Kenneth Lynn), of John
Cheever (by Scott Donaldson), and autobiographies by Emma
Goldman, Maya Angelou, Beryl Markham, others.

'Her health is still good?' I ask Jane.

'She's fine. And what's more, she is all there,' a phrase I take
to mean she is in full possession of her mind.

I like the last sentence of the broadside. How old does she
think she is? Of course she knows. She will live out the rest of
her life in a sterile place where she is one of three patients still
mentally healthy. For her this must be a trial. But her poor
hearing is a blessing. The constant babble and laments of the
forgotten, deserted, and confused do not disturb her.

I will make up a box of books next week. On second
thought, I think I may slip in a carton of cigarettes, and a bottle
of apricot brandy to guarantee her some good nights' sleep.

∽

While I pack books tonight, I consider my passion for collecting
them. During many moves, from Oakland, California, to
Millwood, New York, to Des Moines, Iowa, to Rensselaer and

New Baltimore and Albany, New York, to Washington, D.C., and now, in less than two months, to Maine, I have left behind, or sold, or given away, half of every collection I had. I collect, and dispose, collect again, sometimes, later, buying a book I have just given away or sold only to discover I cannot live without it. The other day I came upon a volume of writings by the sixteenth-century Dutch scholar Erasmus, who described his passion for owning books: 'When I get a little money I buy books; and if any is left, I buy food and clothes.'

This time I have decided to reduce my collection by two-thirds. My single criterion is: Will I ever read this book again? This is a harsh and most difficult rule to observe, for many of the books on my fiction shelves have been given or sent to me, inscribed by the author, and while I read and enjoyed many of them, I know well I will not return to them.

But even as I make my piles—give away to friends, to the Salvation Army, the Vassar book sale, etc.; sell to a dealer of first editions; move to the apartment we will keep in Washington for 'the bad months' (when can they possibly be?); ship to Maine—I am suffering all the triumphs as well as the pains of the true collector. The victory: I am under the impression I have conquered my terrible acquisitiveness. The pain: Even if I think I will not reread them, I am attached to these books, their familiar, fading spines, their width and height. They have been a part of my life for so long that separation from them is loss.

But then I think, perhaps it is time to stop clinging to myself and my 'belongings,' the foolish solipsism that I have always been guilty of, and begin to look outward. If there are to be some good years, I intend to take an elementary course in the moods and changes of Billings Cove, from early morning to the dying light, and then raise my eyes to an advanced study of Eggemoggin Reach beyond the cove, and after that do graduate work on the glory of the surrounding hills and woods. It may be that in this way I will empty my glutted interior self, and fill it with the beauty of a world that is not the self, and never has been.

∽

A funeral today for a young man I knew, whose family announces, in the *New York Times* obituary, that he died of pneumonia. He was twenty-eight, unmarried, worked for a ballet company, and leaves his parents, two sisters, and a brother. No mention of a companion or friend. No mention of what I suspect was the real cause of death. Sad, to be so afraid of the most tragic truth of our time, to call it by another name, and so disassociate oneself and one's frightened family from the life choices and the subsequent agonies of a son.

∽

I suddenly understand why some people become more attentive to dying persons then they were to them in the years of their health. I know two such persons. I suspect they have a deep fear of death. They pay safe little visits to the mortally ill, relish trial contacts with death, enjoy tentative touches to the dry hand of the moribund. From the secure shores of their own health, they observe the last moments, objective witnesses to the permanent fact of death. Standing fully alive at the bedside of the dead, assuring themselves of their own survival, diminishes their terrible fear . . . for the moment.

April

The house is having its chimney lined, for the first time in one hundred years. So far as we know there has never been a fire in it, but still, the inspector for the new owners insists it be done before the sale is complete. The repair man informs us that ninety percent of the chimneys in the District of Columbia are unlined. For the two months we have to live here, we will have the expensive distinction of being among the ten percent who have a lined one.

At the same time we have word from the inspector for the Sargentville house we are purchasing that one chimney for the woodstove is unlined, and the other is crumbling and entirely unsafe. We ask our Maine lawyer to see if the owners will make these repairs, or reduce the price of the house. We are quickly informed they will do neither.

Recently we reroofed the Washington house in preparation for sale. At the same time we learn that the roof on the Maine house is about forty years old and has been therapeutically patched many times. Will the owners consider taking six thousand dollars, the estimated cost of replacing the roof, from the purchase price? They will not.

But none of this financial drain changes my desire to sell the house here, and begin to live in Sargentville. If I once insisted that it was too late for me to lead a totally new life, I may have been right, but I would like to try to prove I was wrong. Very rapidly, we fix all the things here that have needed doing for a long time, small matters like door latches, wallpaper replacement, and ironwork repainting, and expensive things like lining the chimney. The house is now in better condition than it has been since we bought it years ago, a state of affairs that makes Sybil think, in her profound ambivalence, that we ought not to sell it. She wants to stay, she loves the house more than the unknown virtues of Maine. I want to go, fearing the ugly vices of life in a threatened city, and wishing to become acquainted, for the rest of my life, with peace and isolation.

No silence exists for twenty miles around great cities like Washington. The space is occupied by the never-ceasing hum and clatter of machines, air conditioners, whistles, elevators, refrigerators, radios, televisions, the clash of bottles and cans, human voices. Almost nowhere can one detect the sound of insects or birds (one may catch sight of them in parks but they seem to be soundless). They are wiped out by the roar, day and night, of traffic, airplanes, sirens. Immediately beyond the twenty-mile outskirts, the circle of another city touches it—there are almost no places of silence left between cities. The greatest ecological failure in my lifetime has been the loss of quiet, a disappearance as soul-wearying as the dirty junkyard that the industrial, ruined earth has become.

For me there are two saddening consolations. In my youth I trusted the earth to be eternally safe and everlastingly beautiful. The thought of death was bitter, because the fine things I loved in the natural world would go on while I would disappear. Everything beautiful—the pure, enlivening air, the leaves in their metamorphosing glory, the strong, solid Palisades hills and the light-grey waters of the Hudson River, the night (even in Manhattan where I grew up) filled with stars and moonlight, the fresh, brave faces of flowers and the strong, aspiring branches of trees on Riverside Drive, in Van Cortlandt Park, in Central Park (the 'country' of my childhood)—would endure. But I would not be here to see it all.

The consolation: What I so loved has gone, and I may outlive even the little that remains in isolated places far from the cities. The tragedy of modern life is that human beings, for a short time, may be here after natural beauty has disappeared from their earth.

The other consolation: I am slowly losing my hearing, so the omnipresent cacophony is largely lost on me.

Another deprivation: The luxury of ample space has been taken away from us. Too many persons enter the urban world, too fast, and die too slowly. *Lebensraum* has shrunk until we cannot move or turn around without knocking elbows, stumbling over the feet of others, breathing their exhaled breath. The Great Meadow of Central Park is now a sea of bodies and dust. Stretched-out sunbathers on the nation's beaches obscure from view every inch of sand. Mountain roads and national parks have become a trail of campers and live-in cars. Restaurants are fast-food troughs for millions of the population always in motion. Every space is taken, as in a mall parking lot. In cities we are each frozen into the space of our own dimensions, limited to the measurements in life of what will be our containers in death.

∽

I read today that C. S. Lewis thought *A Slip of the Tongue* would be a good title for a short novel. As far as I can tell he never used it. It occurs to me it might also be a suitable title for a memoir.

∽

On television I see Mary McCarthy talking about her Vassar friend, the poet Elizabeth Bishop. I notice Mary's instant, icy smile, so often present when I interviewed her in Paris in 1966 for a book. George Grosz saw the same smile on Lenin's face. 'It doesn't mean a smile,' he said. I am fascinated by it. It represents, I think, an unsuccessful attempt to soften a harsh, bluntly stated judgment. Last summer, twenty-two years after the book I wrote about her, which she so disliked, appeared, I encountered Mary for the first time in an outdoor market in Blue Hill.

'Hello, Mary,' I said. 'Do you remember me?'

Her smile flashed and then, like a worn-out bulb, disappeared instantly.

'Unpleasantly,' she said.

It didn't mean a smile.

∽

I hear from Isaac Wheeler, my grandson, that he is trying to decide on a college to attend in the fall. Sybil, a Swarthmore alumna, hopes he will go there, because she believes his strong social conscience (he is the only teenager on the board of the War Resisters League) will be received hospitably on that campus. Isaac liked his visit to Yale, his father's school. I think it will not matter too much which college he chooses. He is a sensitive, bright, hardworking, inquisitive, talented young man, who loves his family in particular and the human family in general. He will learn wherever he goes. In the process, I hope

he will not lose his scorn for bald ambition, fraud, and
pretension, his vow never to engage in war, his concern for the
displaced, the mistreated, the homeless, the outsiders. At
Stuyvesant High School in New York, he organized a day for
Civil Rights for Gays and Lesbians. He and his friends who
worked with him are not gay, but he thought students should be
made aware of the injustice of such denial to that segment of the
population.

Despite the unpleasant clichés of the doting grandmother
that I try to avoid, I am proud of him. He represents the only
immortality I am likely to achieve. I wish I were leaving him a
more civilized, livable, just, and decent world. But I have faith
that he will do what he can, somehow, to try to improve it.

∽

Today, while there is still money left in my Washington
account, I sent checks to the two artists' colonies I have
attended, Yaddo and MacDowell. Not very large checks, but
something to signify my gratitude for the time and space they
granted me in the past. It is unlikely I shall ever return to them,
because it appears I have at long last acquired a clone of those
blessed places, where I can work undisturbed, can find the peace
that often, for me, produces good prose, and can luxuriate in
uncrowded, private space.

∽

MacDowell: It was the first colony I ever attended, the first time
I knew the virtues of living and working among artists whose
whole attention was focused on their work. MacDowell is on
the outskirts of the small town of Peterborough, New
Hampshire. It is a wooded compound of small cabins for work,
and a few larger buildings for living, eating, playing. There is
communal breakfast, and then a long, almost timeless-seeming

day, unbroken by the presence of anything but oneself, the fire one has built against the early-morning cold, and the lunch basket left quietly on the steps.

Whenever the muse vanished, or inspiration gave out, or my back grew tired of sitting at a typewriter in a camp chair, I would close the damper in the fireplace, pat the growing pile of manuscript fondly, pull the door shut, and take off, in the company of like-minded writers, artists, and composers, for the fire pond, where we swam without the encumbrance of clothing, or a nearby lake (there seemed to be hundreds of them all around us). Dinner was a convivial time, with wine at some tables provided by a more affluent guest. After dinner we talked around the great fireplace in the Hall while some skillful gamesters played an incomprehensible (to me) game called cowboy pool.

Some colonists (as we were called) went into town, where there was one hotel bar, or to a movie house that seemed to show the same film the entire time I was there. Others went back to their studios to work. Still others went early to bed, alone or with a friend, claiming a desire to rise very early and get to work. Whatever it was one did, it was in good company, with good companions, people I was to know from the end of my stay until now.

We wore our oldest and most mismatched clothes at the Colony. I remember only two exceptions to this practice: writer Jerre Mangione, who wore fine suits and a silk ascot at the neck, as befitted the elegant Sicilian he was, and Grace Glueck, who wrote art news for the *New York Times* and dressed in 'outfits,' as they used to be called, everything matching, and wore stockings and heeled shoes while the rest of us shuffled around in sneakers and L. L. Bean woodsman's clothes.

But the work I was able to do in those silent woods! Out of sight of other studios, steeped in the pleasure of knowing I would be entirely alone with whatever was inside me that had to come out, for eight hours. I was in the Baetz Studio on my first visit, working on a novel called *The Missing Person*. It moved along slowly. I could not understand why my progress was not greater. Then I realized that every morning, compulsively, before I started to write, I sat on the cot and read the dedicatory plaque over the fireplace. It said that this studio had been erected in memory of Anna Baehr, nurse to Edward MacDowell during his long, last illness and devoted friend to Marian MacDowell after his death. I can't vouch for the words verbatim (I've never been back to it since that summer), but this was the sense of what was written on the plaque.

One afternoon I walked to the graves of the MacDowells. Carved on a large, impressive stone were their names and their dates, revealing the fact that Marian had survived Edward by almost fifty years. I could not find Anna Baehr's grave. (In the novel I was to bury her at the foot of the MacLarens/MacDowells, with the words LOVE AND DUTY engraved on her small, flat stone.)

Every morning, rereading the plaque, I wondered: Why did the composer die so young, what was the premature illness that Anna Baehr nursed him through, why did Anna stay on, what was her life like at the Colony with Marian, what was Marian's long afterlife like? I became so preoccupied with these questions that, hardly aware of it, I sat on the cot for longer periods of time each morning, making fictions of the three lives, one of whom must have been in the studio I now worked in, at least for its dedication.

I stopped working on *The Missing Person*. My head had filled with invented stories about the MacDowells (now called the MacLarens in my fiction), the nurse, the Colony (moved to Saratoga in the early years of this century to take advantage of the fashionable atmosphere), the people they might have known, the intermingling of their lives and their loves.

In a month I wrote the first half of the story. I finished that draft, another, and then another in other places. But the aura of the Colony was in my head and, I suppose, in my hand when I worked on *Chamber Music*. I believe that without the real place, this could not have happened. My novel belongs to those lovely woods as much as it belongs to me.

∽

Yaddo: On the edge of Saratoga Springs, within earshot of the Northway that runs from Albany to farther upstate New York, it is a colony much in the spirit of MacDowell, but different in that its surroundings are elegant. Most of the guests (here called Fellows) live, literally, in a mansion, left to the colony by Kathryn Trask in memory of her husband and four dead children, all of whose tragic spirits seem to inhabit the large common rooms and many fine, old-fashioned bedrooms. The spacious bathrooms are marble. The veranda looks out on vast lawns and a rose garden, to which the public is invited during the day. But it is separated from the mansion and its lawn by strict signs. Having drinks on the veranda before dinner, and coffee after it, we would look down at people straggling across the lower lawn, looking up at us, and pointing. We felt like some sort of curious aristocracy, not a common experience for writers, painters, composers. It was ego-elevating, it was lovely.

I worked in spaces off my bedroom, once in a room Carson McCullers used, another time in a room in which William Carlos Williams wrote a section of *Paterson*. On my last visit, two years after John Cheever's death, I was given his customary bedroom and study. The first night a small brown bird flew about in the rafters, settled on a bust of Caesar, and left when I opened the screen on a window. I knew who it was: Cheever himself, returned to see who was sleeping in his bed and occupying his desk. I worked well that summer, on *The Magician's Girl,* with the spirit of John Cheever giving me support and courage.

What makes Yaddo, and other colonies, of course, valuable is the company you keep. Here I met John Leggett. My long association with the Iowa Writers Workshop was the result of the afternoon we sat beside the Yaddo pool. He said, 'Have you ever thought of teaching writing?'

'*Writing,*' I said, with all the scorn that a longtime professor of literature can summon up. 'How in the world does one teach writing?'

As I recall, he let that question pass. Instead he asked when I would be able to get a semester off from American University to come to Iowa City. In a year, I thought. So it came about. I have no idea what those workshop students may have learned from me, but I learned the answer to my question. In the long, tough, highly critical workshops held once a week in that happy place, in the presence of those enormously talented students, you simply hold their coats while they go at it.

At Yaddo I met two novelists at the beginning of their careers who are still my friends, Joseph Caldwell and Allan Gurganus. We used to go out drinking together, wandering the fashionable streets in our ragged writer's clothes (although I remember Allan once bought a battered raccoon coat in a secondhand store and wore it at night regardless of the heat). We talked endlessly about what we were writing, sometimes about the other Fellows and their peculiarities. We became friends despite the difference in our ages—I was at least twenty years older than they. The bond of a common endeavor and the fine, relaxed time after the day's work wiped out, at least for me, that disparity. And still does.

∽

Now that I know we are soon leaving these Washington streets, I find myself walking more often. There have been weeks when I have not used the car. Serendipitously last night, Sybil brought home a seventeenth-century book by Thomas Fuller, *The Holy State*. I read here and there in it (I am not fond of religious tracts) and found a fine sentence: 'Running, leaping, and dancing, the descants on the plainsong of walking, are all excellent exercise.'

Aha. If I am certain I am not being watched, and because I am so excited by the thought of moving to Maine shortly, I may take to running, leaping, and dancing along North Carolina Avenue to the market, the post office, and Wayward Books. Occupied in this way, I may even stop counting my steps.

May

*T*he first stage of the move was accomplished today. Most of our 'city' furniture, some of our books, and half of our kitchen and linen supplies are now in an apartment on C Street, around the corner from the bookstore and across the street from the Eastern Market. It is small, but has two balconies which give it a more ample sense. However, one of them looks out at a distant row of trees which will soon be obscured by the upper stories of a corner building to be erected in the summer. The study is a small, viewless room we will share, since Sybil has a computer like mine and will bring it from the store when we return here in the winter.

I have not lived in an apartment for almost twenty years. There is something odd about going home to a lobby, an elevator, another hallway, and then a series of boxes opening into one another, with the same doors, the same fixtures, and two identical bathrooms, the only difference between them being the location of the toilet-paper holder.

Our furniture, rearranged a number of times, and our books all seem to be cramped into these rooms. This is true city living, too much furnishing, too little space. A symbol of the reduction is the absence of the sixteen volumes of the *Oxford English Dictionary,* soon to be making their way on the van to Maine, and the substitution of the two-volume edition, with its 2-point print and magnifying glass.

∽

A handsome young black man comes to install our two telephone lines. It takes a long time to bring the extra line in. He rests now and then, and looks at the walls of books.

'Have you read all these?'

'Most of them.'

'What do you do?'

'I write.'

'I've often thought of being a writer.'

'Why?'

'Oh, to make more money. And to sit down while I work.'

'I think you may make more money doing what you do. And I get tired of sitting down.'

'You're kidding. And another reason—you get famous and people recognize you on the street.'

'Not really. Only if you're Norman Mailer or Stephen King or someone like that.'

'Who is Norman Mailer?'

'A famous writer.'

'Oh. Well, both phones are now working. I enjoyed the talk.'

'Thank you. So did I. If you became a writer what would you like to write about?'

'Anything, anything that makes money. My life, maybe. Well, so long.'

June and July

*M*aine. In the bookstore van, we start on our way from Washington to Sargentville, stopping to visit the Kosteckis, Sybil's family outside Philadelphia. There I am given her granddaughter Rachael's bedroom. The walls are papered with photographs of a boy who appears, I gather, in soap operas. He is Rachael's love. Her bed had been covered with stuffed animals, now thoughtfully removed for me. I lie on it for some time before I go to sleep, the light on, trying to imagine, or remember, what it was like to be adolescent, protected from my family and the outside world by a wall of toys and pictures of . . . who was pasted on my wall then? John Gilbert?

We stop the next evening at Jim Hillman's house in Connecticut, for an hour in his hot tub, a good dinner, much loud talk between argumentative male guests and the host, and sleep. Then it is time to make the last part of the journey north to 'Plas Newydd,' as the heroines of *The Ladies* called their house in Wales: the New Place. But we have decided against calling our house Plas Newydd or even Serious Trouble. It will be the Captain White House, because that is the name painted

on our mailbox. We know little about Captain White, but there
is a comfortable sense of anonymity and buried history behind
the name, so we shall keep it.

The moving van with our furniture and books is traveling a
faster, more direct route toward Sargentville. One of the
moving men is driving Troilus, my car, loaded with electronic
equipment, bed pillows, and boxes of food. I have stayed in the
new apartment for a few nights, not long enough to be able to
think of it as another home. 'Home' will keep, until we travel
for three days, six states, 750 miles, and pull into the driveway
of the Captain White House.

This move is not without its anxieties for me. One of the
most constant is the worry that the view, for which I know we
bought the place, will grow dull, static, without interest, after
we have looked out at it for a time. Another is that I will not be
able to convey my muse from the wondrous little carriage house
to the room in Maine I have chosen for a study because its view
of the cove is so fine. In less elevated terms, that I won't be able
to write here.

'Convey' is a real estate word I have acquired in the last
months. We put into our contract a notice that the
tin-and-copper chandelier in the carriage house 'does not
convey.' Cynthia Graae, once a writing student of mine, is the
purchaser, with her husband Steven. She loves the carriage house
as I do, wants to use it to write, and asked if the muse conveyed.

I suspect my doubts are at the bottom of the dream I had last
night at Jimmy's, summarizing all my old anxieties. It is the
beginning of the winter semester. I am about to teach a class of
eight students, the only ones who have shown up out of an
enrollment of thirty-five. I can't remember what the course is. I
find a paper on my desk which informs me it is Advanced
Accounting. Then I discover I have forgotten to wear a blouse. I
rush to the back of the room while the *real* teacher takes the

roll. I gather up my bookbag and escape to a room marked FAC
ULTY. A tall nun looks in and tells me I don't belong there. I
leave, forgetting my purse. When I get to my car, still partially
dressed, I discover I do not have my car keys (they are in the
purse). A long search begins for the the faculty room. I need the
purse; it has my money in it. I am frightened because I
remember I have to call my mother to tell her I'll be late.

My dream is full of familiar worries from my past. No one
will want to take my course. I am unprepared to teach it
properly. In my rush not to be late, I have forgotten some
necessary article of clothing. I am really not qualified to be a
member of a faculty. I will lose everything I need. My mother
will worry because I am not home on time. I cannot call her.

A fleeting moment of pleasure comes as I wake, perspiring,
from the terrors I have experienced. I have had a glimpse of my
mother's concerned face. She is young and handsome,
black-haired and blue-eyed, a beautiful woman whom I loved
and who worried about me. But the memory is gone quickly. I
am fully awake and flooded with apprehension. What will
happen if the place we have bought is uncomfortable, cold, if
the furniture does not fit, if the roof leaks, if the cellar is wet, if
the view of the cove begins to pale?

I will telephone my mother, who has been dead for thirty-three
years, and tell her that I don't like it here and I will be home as soon
as I find my purse. Or maybe I will ask her to come and get me and
take me home.

∽

We arrive at the house after noon, almost at the same time as the
moving van. The ground, frozen and hard when we had our
'walk-through' in April before the closing, is now a morass of
mud. The van proceeds down our driveway and immediately
sinks into it. Fortunately Ted and Bob have come to meet us

and know the proper fellow with a tractor to call. Chains are
applied, the van is freed. It is almost three hours, and getting
dark, before the moving men can begin to bring in the furniture
and cartons. Their tempers shorten; the sixty cartons of books
are no longer the light matter they were when they loaded them
in Washington. They leave with their check, glad to be gone
from us and our treacherous mudhole of an estate.

We are here, not yet home, but here. We eat the dinner our
friends have brought, make the bed, and get into it gratefully,
not very reassured by the events of the day, too weary to build a
case for optimism. Tonight I am so tired that I have no dreams
of disaster, no dreams at all. I sleep until five, when I am
awakened by a loud thumping outside the window, and
discover that two blue jays have landed on the bird feeder
erected by the former owners outside our window.

∽

The first morning. We watch the sky lighten as we lie in bed.
The water turns from black to blue to green. By six-thirty we
are downstairs, having coffee made in our old pot and staring
from the kitchen window at a new, transformed view of
Billings Cove. But it is very early to be up. We vow to take the
bedroom bird feeder down as soon as possible. Sybil reminds me
of her former sister-in-law who taught a preschool class and
liked to educate her pupils in bird lore. She maintained a feeder
for their instruction. Her dislike of jays communicated itself
successfully to them. One day a little boy rushed into her
classroom and reported: 'Mrs. Hillman, the fucking jays are back
again.'

∽

Our contractor, Tracy Sampson, who has done all the painting
inside the house, reconstructed the study, built an island in the

kitchen, and is now engaged in various electrical and carpentry chores, arrives at nine. The gas man delivers his two canisters of natural gas, the oil man fills our tank, Don Hale, our neighbor who picks up the trash, comes on his first visit to remove packing boxes. We start the endless task of unpacking while Tracy's assistant puts together the bookcases and we begin to fill them.

I would be happy merely to thrust books into shelves to reduce the number of cartons, but the librarian in Sybil will not permit such unprofessional arrangements. Fiction must be shelved alphabetically, the rest of the collection according to subject. I sigh but accept her edict. The emptying of boxes proceeds much more slowly.

∽

First indication of a new environment: Our mailbox is across a rather busy main road. Traffic, we discover, travels at forty-five miles an hour. Sybil is worried. In two weeks, when she returns to her job at the Library of Congress and to the bookstore, she thinks I will be almost instantly killed crossing the road to get letters and the *New York Times,* which I am having delivered by mail.

We questioned the former owners about this weighty matter. They reported they had asked for the box be moved to their side of the road, without success. So they trained their children to *listen* for cars, and then dart swiftly across.

We decide to ask again. The Sargentville post office is in a corner of a private house less than a mile from us, a little cubicle of a place with a devoted postmistress who introduces herself at once to us as Frances. We introduce ourselves to her, but it is unnecessary. She knows our names, where we have come from, exactly when we moved in ('Saw the van coming to work,' she says), knows we are having work done in the house, hopes we

will like it up here. 'Folks from away generally do,' she says. It
is the first time we have heard that phrase, used for anyone not a
born Mainer.

Having been instructed to stand back, say nothing, and look
a bit daft, I do so, while Sybil explains to Frances that she would
be grateful if the mailbox could be moved. 'My friend,' she says,
'is somewhat deaf and may not hear the traffic when it
approaches. And she is no longer able to dart across the road
ahead of it.' Her implication is that those two difficulties are
only the beginning. There are my mental infirmities. I continue
my look of somewhat dazed antiquity, and say nothing.

Frances, herself a lady of a certain age, studies me. Then she
says: 'I think it can be arranged. I'll speak to the postmaster at
Sedgwick [the town nearest to us, and a larger station] and to
the postman.' The next day she telephones to say that both
gentlemen have agreed to the change. The postman will dig up
the letter box himself and replant it at our driveway. In a few
days it is done, civilly and without any further reminder, thus,
to Sybil's way of thinking, saving my life.

∾

Reading has taken on a new quality for me. Before I left
Washington I told my editor/producer that I would be doing
no more reviews for National Public Radio. I had collected
what seemed to me to be good reasons for retiring from the job
I had held for more than five years. Maine was far from
Washington and required long travel in order to tape; I have
grown tired of having to have an opinion on every book I read;
I am losing my hard-won fluency of speech, and the fear that I
will stammer or slip or mispronounce has grown to the point
that every review is both a challenge to perform and an
expectation of failure. In the past, I have had a series of
reassuring editors who helped me through these self-doubts. But

the new chap, very nice but even more nervous than I am, serves only to make me do badly.

I've noticed that persons on radio or television who make one slip of the tongue will invariably make another in the next few sentences. This happened to me at my last taping. So I gave up the difficult monthly chore that I had come to dread, said goodbye to my friends at the station, and left, feeling unburdened and free. I told Alice Winkler not to bother to forward mail or books, another gain that will cut down on correspondence, invitations, and thank-you notes for inscribed books I did not request and could not figure out what to do with.

⌒

Before I left Washington, I asked the post office to return all books sent to me. I wrote to thirty publishers who had been good enought to provide me with their books for review, asking them not to send them any longer. Now, in Sargentville, my mail is reduced to human scale. I am no longer troubled by the arrival, every day, of ten and more brown-boxed books, the disposal of wrappings, the perusal, even scantily, of their contents, and the close reading of two or three for every one I had airtime to review.

My sense of relief is immense. I bought a thirty-six-volume set of Charles Dickens recently—each novel divided into two, three, or four most satisfying little volumes—and have begun *Bleak House,* sitting in a chair on our thick, green lawn, and taking not a single note as I read.

⌒

The lawn: A miraculous transformation has taken place, between April when we came to Maine to 'close' on the house, and now. What appeared to be a large expanse of shredded wheat, dead,

crisp, brown, extending from the driveway and sweeping
around the house and down to the high meadow before the
cove, has metamorphosed into soft, green lawn. Tracy and her
helpers mowed it before we came back, because it had grown
high enough to harbor hordes of black flies and mosquitoes.

We are both charmed at the sight and horrified, having
vowed never to own a lawn mower again in our lives, disliking
the smell the machine creates, the noise it makes. Now we are
faced with a choice: to allow the lawn to go to seed and sow it
with barley, wild flowers, wheat (not shredded) or rye, or to
have someone come to tend the surprising greensward.

∽

I wake at six to a glorious sky, go down to make coffee, open a
front door. For reasons of providing an ample sea view the
house is built on a sort of staggered system, so we have *two* front
doors, one slightly back from the other. The air is cold. It seems,
after the pollution of Washington, to be *original* air, so I breathe
deeply and think: I am home. Suddenly I know what to do
about the lawn. I will go to a flea market and find an
old-fashioned lawn mower, the kind you push, the kind that
easily clogs with grass cuttings, the kind that stops dead in the
presence of stones and sticks, the kind that makes no odor and
very little noise. Little by little I will keep the lively-looking
grass cut. At the same time I will be getting the exercise I badly
need. Double-dipping. Tracy tells me that cutting grass is as
good as playing tennis for that purpose. A dangerous state of
self-satisfaction settles over me.

∽

The dirtiest words spoken in Hancock County: land developer.
One enterprising fellow bought up a large parcel of land on
beautiful and beloved Blue Hill, a handsome mountain about

ten miles from us, put in a road, and began to build what
promised to be a complex of little houses. His plan was to
'develop' the town. Consternation overtook the inhabitants,
who never before had felt the need or the desire to zone the
area. His activities were stopped by injunction, to gain time for
the town to confer about legal means to stop development. This
is the state of things now: a half-finished house, a half-used road,
and angry looks on the countenances of year-round Mainers
whenever they raise their eyes to the half-accomplished work of
the (grimace) land developer.

∽

We buy two local papers, both of which come out on Thursday,
the *Ellsworth American,* conservative in opinion but well written
and well edited, and Blue Hill's *Weekly Packet,* slim and
determinedly parochial. Natives and visitors buy them to keep
abreast of local news and for the announcements of library sales,
church sales, garage sales, yard sales, and flea markets that are
omnipresent and bountiful on weekends.

I read the *Packet* for its illuminating accounts of town
meetings. This week there is an extensive report of a special one
held in Sedgwick on June 8, two weeks ago. The proposal: to
authorize our selectmen 'to trade in the present grader and
backhoe/loader.' Twenty-three interested Sedgwick residents
attended, to 'rehash,' in 'lively' fashion (the words of the printed
account), what had been said at the town meeting in March.

I was not, of course, present in March, being at that time still
'from away' (as I always will be, of course), nor was I alert
enough to be aware of this meeting, but the reporter made it up
to me. Why, asked Ray Carter, was the town getting rid of the
loader? Butch Gray asked why the equipment purchased just
two years ago, the grader in particular, was no longer any good.

The responses by selectmen were both autocratic and

irrelevant. To Ray Carter, Brian Perkins replied that they were authorized to sell equipment, and further, authorized to buy new equipment. To Butch Gray, the road commissioner said: 'When the equipment was bought two years ago, it needed repairs and no repairs were made.'

If the grader was traded in, Jerry Kelly wanted to know, how could the Carter Point Road be graded with a backhoe? Would the town need to buy a new grader? 'The old pull-behind grader would be adequate for grading dirt roads,' said Carter. But 'it does not have enough weight' for other grading, someone pointed out, and further, if the newer road grader is not broken down why is it being replaced? Butch Gray remembered that they had bought the grader for snow removal and ditching and wondered why we had bought it in the first place. Said Ray Carter, the present grader can not plow snow nor can it be used for ditching 'due to a broken part.'

There was more talk, mostly about costs, trade-ins, etc., but the proposal to trade in the grader and backhoe loader was approved. Six voters abstained, apparently having been unable to make up their minds.

But this did not end the matter. Someone asked: 'Is the present backhoe/loader so bad that it cannot be used?' Turns out the equipment in question is sixteen years old with a life expectancy of ten thousand hours. It needs three thousand dollars' worth of repairs. 'Is it unsafe?' someone else inquired. The road commissioner put an end to all further argument. 'Yes. The brakes and ball bearings have not functioned for two years.'

The meeting ended with the unanimous passage of a puzzling (to me) article that required very little discussion: 'to establish a perpetual care fund for a lot in the Camp Stream Cemetery.' For whom? Why? I mean to inquire of my selectman about this matter at the next town meeting.

∽

I like this town. Sargentville is ruled by Sedgwick, being too small to have a government of its own. It has a post office, a general store with a gas station, a veterinarian, and a place to leave UPS packages. I sympathize with its major concerns— roads, snow removal, a new school, the town landing and ramp, raw sewage, taxes, fire equipment, and other similar, vital matters. Like its post office, it operates within the range of my very limited comprehension of matters of government (I failed the Civics Regents in high school). It appears to serve my needs. It is not too big to lose sight of me and our property in its considerations, should I require such concern.

∽

We are becoming acquainted with our cove. It is full of clam and mussel shells, and we think about collecting mussels and going clamming. But Tracy warns us to check with the Sedgwick environmental agency to be sure the red tide is not still a threat. We decide against such activity this year.

The rocks and flats, the coast across from us, the trees at the edge, and the long line of stones that, at low tide, separates the cove from the deepwater mooring (Sybil has noticed it resembles a crocodile) are all lovely. As soon as Sybil returns for her vacation in August we intend to launch Lenore Straus's old canoe loaned to us by Peggy. We wish to make a journey of inspection around the cove to Eggemoggin Reach, a body of water running parallel to our beach and connecting Penobscot and Blue Hill bays. Apparently that is what a 'reach' is. On clear days we see to the reach and beyond, to the low green shores of Deer Isle.

∽

Shall I miss the alley life that my carriage-house windows
supervised in Washington? I think not. At first we found it
amusing to oversee the lengthy fights and loud arguments of the
chaps who lived across from us. They had a pool in their
backyard that I often envied, and a Jacuzzi, both of which were
used mostly in the early hours of the morning. Years ago,
during the time our house was being renovated and we used the
carriage house to live in, their fiery activities, with other young
men who bathed and swam and flirted and fought, kept us
awake.

After we moved out and into the main house, things seemed
to quiet down back there. The property was sold, and the new
owners were a decorous and sedate couple. But often during hot
afternoons I would walk away from my desk to cool off,
vicariously, watching Ron splashing around in the pool, and his
wife standing still at the shallow end reading the *Washington
Post*.

I will not miss my voyeuristic experience of those gay
young men's watery lives, or the sounds of our neighbor's two
young boys. Our wall was contiguous to theirs. We heard
rather than saw the children grow up. The smaller of the boys
was what Sybil termed a screamer. At all hours of the night he
would wake in, apparently, a state of terror, and cry for a long
time. Nothing seemed to quiet him. We never found out
whether he had terrible dreams or whether his older brother
provoked him, or what caused his nightly fright.

But here there are no neighbors, no human sounds that are
not my own (at a distance I am told the traffic hum can be
heard, but not by my failing ears), no sights but the wonderful,
calm sea and the woods on every side. How does one measure
the boundless wonder of such isolation? What are fitting words
of gratitude to have found such a haven, a hermitage, a place of
quiet privacy and solitary silence?

∽

National Public Radio is still airing tapes of reviews I did last month. In the market I meet a chap who is behind me in line. He hears me speak to a clerk, and recognizes my voice.

'Are you Doris Grumbach?' he asks.

'I am.'

'Well, I want to tell you. I listen to you in the morning on the radio while I pee.'

I thank him, thinking that this must be as much fame as I will ever achieve. What greater recognition can come to me? I pay the clerk, who is now staring at me, for the cooking sherry and ginger root I have bought, and leave, quickly.

∽

Late this afternoon, at low tide, I walk down to the edge of the cove. Two small sailboats are anchored in the deep water; a few unpeopled houses dot the shore across the way. The cove is solitary. Trees, rocks, water, a few gulls, a single cormorant drying himself off on the snout of the crocodile rock formation, a family of ducks trailing from Jeannie Wiggins's side of the cove across ours to Rebecca Peterson's, but nothing else. And no one anywhere in sight.

Low tide: It makes me think of the great controversy on Moody Beach twenty years ago. At that time it was a small family beach, inhabited by middle-class owners who were fiercely protective of their property, not only against the assaults of the ocean on their sand and seawalls, but also against the invasion of day visitors who walked across 'their' sand from the public beach and throughway, put down their chairs and towels, and stretched themselves out to sunbathe, swim, have their lunch, and often their dinners, cooked over the little fires they built.

Most owners resented these uninvited guests, because they regarded the entire strip of beach in front of their houses as exclusively their own. But the most deeply offended was a man whose house stood at the very edge of the public beach. For years he tried every means he could think of to keep invaders from crossing 'his' beach, sitting on it, dropping their trash there. He erected a fence; the beach cleaners took it down. He put up a long chain; walkers stepped on it until it broke. He built a wooden barrier; one night someone burned it down.

The law offered him no protection. It clearly held that owners of shore property owned only down to the high-water mark. We left Moody Beach after many happy summers there with our children, so I have no idea what became of that fellow, or if he is the same fellow who made history last year. A suit was won before Maine's Superior Court declaring that property holders now owned down to the *low*-water mark, thus preventing trespassers from walking, sitting, and sunning themselves on 'private' beaches unless they wished to do these things while submerged in water.

This decision is still widely debated in Maine. To many, the right of citizenry to walk the seashore should be assumed, never questioned. I remember my fury, years ago, trying to get to the beach of the Atlantic Ocean, in a city named Miami *Beach,* and discovering that one hotel after another had fenced off its shore space so that passage along the edge of the water was impossible. Further, if I entered the beach area through a hotel and sat down on the sand, I would be asked to leave, unless I was able to produce a towel of the hotel's color, proving I was one of its guests.

I know well: Should I see someone clamming or walking on the shore of the cove I would do nothing, having decided that no one (or everyone) owns my part of the coast, a decision made firmer by a discovery I made after I moved here. Three of the five Maine judges who were responsible for the infamous decision are seashore property owners. There is much talk of an appeal.

Odd. In the years during which we came to Moody Beach no one anywhere seemed to have heard of the place. Now, everywhere, the name immediately brings glares and sneers to the faces of inland Mainers. Shorefront owners, on the other hand, grow very quiet when the Moody Beach law is discussed.

∽

I have become a member of a very small communion of Episcopalians who meet for services in the American Legion Hall in Blue Hill. Most of them are sturdy, healthy retirees, professionals who have left cities all over the country and moved to this peninsula to live out their lives. There is not a black, Hispanic, or Oriental face among them. Through this homogeneous church, the thirty or so families have become friends as well as parishioners. After Sunday-morning Eucharistic service, they stay to have coffee and cakes and to talk about the 'outreach' programs many of them engage in. One works in an old people's home on Saturdays, another is active in a program to build houses for homeless families, one is concerned with helping Hancock's adult illiterates learn to read. On the whole, they are well-to-do and extremely active. I am of the belief that Maine residents live a long time because, unlike Florida retirees, they rarely sit down. They walk, sail, garden, shop, go to the library, the post office, the bookstore, visit and assist their friends, go to restaurants, movies, concerts, lectures, classes in crafts. Yesterday I heard a neighbor talking about a friend in Camden who had died, 'prematurely,' she said. Turned out the gentleman was eighty-one. Not to reach ninety up here is regarded as a disappointing act of carelessness or accident. The slogan here seems to be the old German saw *Rast ich, so rost ich.* When I rest, I rust.

The church is named St. Francis by the Sea. The congregation's style of worship might be called 'low'; the spirit of unity is noticeable. We sit on camp chairs put up for the morning, and only a very few persons kneel, although cushions are stacked at the door for such use. Never have I heard so few voices sing so lustily, make such a joyful noise unto the Lord, as the Psalmist writes.

Everyone seems to play some part in the life of the mission church, as it is called because it is too small to be a parish. Most people contribute to the service or the coffee hour afterwards. Unlike some congregations this one includes no children. The youngest participant is the crucifer, aged about fourteen; the oldest, Jennie Learned, is ninety-five and almost blind. She is helped to her seat by two ushers. Her small but true voice can be heard singing clearly the hymns she knows by heart.

The congregation talks of trying to find space of its own, either by building a church, buying a building and converting it, or renting permanent space. People wonder if they can afford such a luxury, especially since the rector, whom they share with Castine and Deer Isle, is about to retire and they would like a full-time priest to replace him.

I like this little church. Not having a consecrated space of its own, worshiping perforce in the cave of the militant American Legion (the creed of the Auxiliary, mounted on the wall and covered with a sheet during church time, promises to support soldiers and veterans in wars in which the country, right or wrong, engages), it reminds me of early Christianity under Rome when a few gathered together somewhere in His Name. . . .

In Washington, the church I attend is at the other end of the ecclesiatical spectrum, very 'high,' Anglo-Catholic, full of lovely, almost lavish rituals, flowers, incense sprinkled at every stage of the rite, bells rung often, almost constant kneeling and crossing of oneself, music that leans heavily on chant, daily masses, all in one of the most beautiful small church buildings in the city, surrounded by a fine garden. Worshiping at St. James is an aesthetic experience. The congregation is experienced in shuffling through the many booklets of liturgy, musical-response sheets, church bulletins, and more in order to follow the complex liturgy. The priest, Father Downing, is dedicated and earnest; some of the more worshipful parishioners bow to him as he passes in procession at the beginning and end of the mass. The congregation, a heterogeneous blend of black and white faces with a liberal sprinkling of homosexuals, is active in the community, especially in serving the needs of AIDS patients in the hospital next door, the poor down the street, the homeless in the city.

This disparity of persons, methods of worship, and physical surroundings is characteristic of the admirable variety that exists in the Episcopal Church. The clergy themselves differ on major matters, especially the pressing question of the ordination of women, and the even more distressing (to some) elevation of a woman (who happens also to be black) to suffragan bishop. When this happened, our liberal priest at St. James announced the event from the altar and asked the congregation to sing a Te Deum in celebration. Visiting that Sunday was a retired priest from South Africa. As we filed out I shook his hand and said: 'A great day, isn't it, bishop?'

He responded glumly: 'Not quite so for all of us. Good morning.'

Sunday. A beautiful day. My resolution to be firm in the
practice of my faith weakens in the presence of the sunshine on
our new deck, which spreads out across the windows and door
from my study and cantilevers toward the cove. So I stay home,
and walk down to explore the berry bushes that are flowering in
our muddle of a meadow, the little patch of blueberry bushes
that hug the ground, the myriad wildflowers growing
everywhere, anonymously. I have no idea what they are called,
but I intend to search out their names. Could one be sleepwort?
Ironweed?

I use Richard's ash cane to walk toward the water. Sybil
follows me down with leftover pieces of treated wood from the
finished deck and builds four steps into the still muddy bank to
make my descent easier. We test the water and find it is still
cold. 'Freezing,' she says. 'Cool,' I call it. I cannot wait to swim
in it, but Sybil insists I will have to buy her a fur-lined wet suit
before she will do more than test it with her toe.

We have lunch on the deck, celebrating the new space and
the absence of omnivorous black flies and ubiquitous
mosquitoes. Sybil goes off to tramp around the acre that will
hold the bookstore we are planning to build and a new
driveway to it, while I struggle with the last pages of *Camp*. It
seems strange to be recreating fictionally the adolescent sadness
of my fourteenth year in this luminous place that has, in some
ways, changed my dolorous thinking. The first drafts were
finished in the winter before we found the Captain White House.

There is a settled permanency about a completed manuscript
that takes on the coloration of the place, the house, the room, in
which it was written, at least in the writer's mind. I came to
Maine too late to do anything, good or bad, for *Camp,* except
perhaps to have it keep this memoir company as it goes forth
into the cold and critical world.

~

I discover that Jennie Learned, the elderly presence in our church, is the mother of Anne Chamberlyn, a Washington acquaintance. Anne tells me her nonagenarian mother is taking singing lessons from a local tenor. I think of Zelda Fitzgerald's desire to *begin* dancing (ballet) well into her thirties, and a friend's sister who was still studying to make her *debut* in opera when she was over sixty. The tenor, who used to run the luncheonette in Blue Hill, coaches Mrs. Learned in the music being sung by her choral group because she cannot read it.

I remember Edith Hamilton *began* to write her superb books on mythology, Rome, and Greece after she was forced, at sixty-five, to retire from her job as headmistress of the Bryn Mawr School. Harriet Doerr wrote her fine first novel, *The Stones of Ibarra,* in her early seventies. 'How old would we be if we didn't know how old we was?' Peggy, thinking, I believe, of her good friend Lenore, the sculptor, says she thinks we die only when our work is done. I would like to think that is true. I have work still to do, I think.

~

Today I was asked to be a lector in church. The prospect of it made me nervous all week. I practiced every morning, reading from the Lectionary the two epistles assigned to this Sunday. One, Paul's letter to the Hebrews, the beginning of the thirteenth verse, I like very much. 'Let brotherly love continue,' he wrote. 'Do not neglect to show hospitality to strangers, for thereby some have entertained angels unawares.' But even my fondness for the selection did not calm my usual fears about stammering. It helped a little to remember Spencer Tracy's advice on acting: 'Just know your lines and don't bump into the furniture.'

∽

I have recovered the sight of the horizon. In Washington it is invisible, sunk behind hills, houses, monuments, government buildings. But here, driving to the post office, I catch sight of it on my right because the reach runs behind the houses, the houses are far apart, and, where the water meets the sky, the horizon displays itself at every turn.

Driving the other road, up Caterpillar Hill, I see 365 degrees of horizon, a heartening sight for a lover of that thin grey unending line. I wonder if it could be true that, as someone once wrote (I cannot remember the author), death itself is a horizon, and a horizon is only the limit of our sight.

∽

Some time back in this journal I berated the women on an airplane for their blue-jeaned, uniformlike clothes. Now, as I look about me on the streets and in the stores of Blue Hill and Ellsworth, I see how biased those reproaches were. Here everyone wears a discernible uniform, men and women alike. We are all dressed in clothes bought from L. L. Bean's, with a few variations ordered from the catalogues of Eddie Bauer or Land's End. Sweaters, pants, shoes, socks, shirts, caps, jackets: all alike, differing only in size and color, and places of origin. Our unvarying grey or white hair adds to the impression that we are all members of a platoon, marching to the same inflexibly demanding drummer time.

∽

Early this morning, after the post office, I stopped at the general store near our house to buy a bran-apple-raisin muffin. A chap I have never seen comes in very early every morning and bakes them 'fresh,' as they say. It is a good place to listen to people on their way to work—carpenters, painters, ground-clearers, road repairmen (with backhoe or grader, I suppose), delivery chaps, trash removers, berry pickers, gardeners—talk about local matters, using phrases that stump me.

Today the talk is about the weather. It has been very, very dry for two weeks, until today.

'Doesn't amount to Hannah Cook,' I hear someone say about the rain.

'What does that mean?' I ask a handsome, elderly fellow customer who is also buying muffins. He was the right one to ask, it turned out. He is a gentleman-sailor with a boat harbored at the neck of Billings Cove.

'It means worthless, the way a cook on board ship is no good for navigation. Never heard it used except in Maine.'

When I get home I look it up in every book of idioms I can find, without success. 'A hill of beans' is there, but not Maine's Hannah Cook.

◊

The telephone book for the Blue Hill/Ellsworth area is one-half inch thick. This includes both white and yellow pages. Washington's population and business phones require two volumes, three inches in thickness. This is one of the differences between my life in the city, and this one here: two and one-half inches of people and places.

◊

Three old acquaintances of mine have died since we moved to Maine: I. F. Stone, Sidney Hook, and Howard Simons.

Izzie and I shared an office at American University for two years. He had become known to the English department because he used the library in the preparation of his book on Socratic politics. Although he never taught, he was offered space in which to work.

It was a fine time for me. My Attic Greek was very rusty, and here was a seventy-two-year-old fellow, with very bad eyesight and a history of heart attacks, teaching himself the language so he could approach Plato and Euripides in their own tongue. He would ask me questions of vocabulary, and I realized that forty-five irregular Greek verbs had entirely vanished from my once-reliable memory. He had the enthusiasm, pixielike grin, and energy of a boy, and a fierce determination to learn that made other academics seem weak and languid. He lived to publish his iconoclastic study of the Athenians' treatment of Socrates, to much critical interest. At this moment he is probably hard at work learning a celestial language in order to argue metaphysics with Thomas Aquinas.

Sidney Hook taught me in three philosophy courses at New York University. He was a brilliant teacher, persuading me that philosophy was the only academic enterprise worth engaging in. For two years I majored in his department. Then I changed to medieval literature under Margaret Schlauch's influence. From then on he treated me with some coldness, even pointing out at the Phi Beta Kappa induction that he never knew anyone, except Maggie, who approached political thought with such complete illogic. Once again our paths crossed when I asked him to review a book for *The New Republic*.

For a few years he was pleasant. Then we fell out again. A book of his appeared. He wrote, suggesting that Lewis Feuer, then in Canada, be asked to review it. Ordinarily I did not take kindly to authors who suggested their own reviewers but, still somewhat in awe of the famous professor, I wrote to Feuer. The Canadian postal service was on strike; the letter, so far as I knew, was lost. At all events, Feuer never responded, time passed, and then it was too late to review the book. Sidney Hook never spoke to me again.

But I remember him with gratitude. He taught me how to think about a question, how to state a thesis, how to know what evidence I would regard as disproof of the proposition, how to argue logically. I remember the admirable words he wrote after his entry in the latest *Who's Who in America:* 'Man's vocation should be the use of the arts of intelligence in behalf of human freedom.'

And Howard Simons: a lovely, intelligent, gentle journalist in whose parents' house I and my children lived during the Berlin Crisis so we could be in Albany while my husband was 'called up' into the Medical Corps. I looked Howard up when I came to Washington. He had become a noted science writer for the *Washington Post* and then its even more famous managing editor, the fellow who sent Bernstein and Woodward to the Watergate to look into a break-in at Democratic national headquarters. He was a lovable, witty fellow who once wrote a parody of a scientist's research paper that proved heaven was at least seventy-five degrees Celsius hotter than hell. I trust he is up there now, preparing to investigate the truth of his mockery.

And yet: Izzie was almost eighty, Sidney Hook was eighty-six, Howard Simons was sixty. This spring we invited David, a friend and one of the finest hairdressers in Washington, to lunch on our deck. A slight, sweet-natured fellow, he spent an afternoon a week at Capitol Hill Hospital cutting the hair of AIDS patients. Now, he told us, he was struggling with the terrible affliction. His hope was that his new doctor, with an 'innovative' treatment, would be able to help him.

The last time I saw David, when I stopped into his shop to tell him we were going to Maine, he was standing quietly behind his chair cleaning his instruments. He said he was leaving his job. Now we hear he is in the hospital, very ill. Sybil says she will call when she gets back to Washington next week. David is thirty-four years old.

∽

The town of Blue Hill had a Thomas Jefferson–like early settler. Jonathan Fisher, whose house is now a historical memorial, came to Blue Hill at the very end of the eighteenth century. He had studied at Harvard, both liberal arts and divinity, and established the Congregational church in the town. He and his parishioners built his house, which he designed. He read Hebrew, Latin, and Greek and taught these languages to students who boarded with him. He was a skilled painter, draftsman, and wood engraver. To augment his meager pastor's salary, he farmed his own acres, braided straw hats, concocted 'medicinal remedies,' carved buttons out of animal bones, made pumps, chairs, chests, combs, tables, bureaus, and drumsticks for the local militia. He wrote poetry and several books, founded a school and a library, went on missionary journeys, spoke out for bettering the lot of Negroes, surveyed property, and fathered seven children.

All these facts are taken from a brochure the novelist Mary Ellen Chase compiled for the use of the museum. She was an inhabitant of Blue Hill, was proud of the town and of Jonathan Fisher. The town seems to be proud of them both. It is good to think that men like Thomas Jefferson, Benjamin Franklin, and Jonathan Fisher are our true ancestors, Renaissance men who, more than generals, politicians, and 'developers,' represent the early American love of art and learning we seem now to be losing.

∽

The postmistress, Frances, says she noticed a road had been cut into our property. Frances misses very little that happens in Sargentville. I tell her, yes, we are preparing to move Wayward

Books up here into a new building on the acre within sight of our house. Perhaps we will call it Wayward Books Downeast, I tell her. She seems pleased.

She gives me a huge bundle of mail. In it is a letter from a friend in Los Angeles, to whom I wrote about my new house. She sends me a clipping about Dylan Thomas, who spent the last four years of his life in the tiny seaside village of Laugharne in South Wales. He lived in a boathouse, which he called 'my seashaken house on a breakneck of rock,' now a museum. Above it is a small shedlike building, which he called his 'wordsplashed hut.' It overlooks the bay and, according to the newspaper report, is in danger of sliding off the cliff into the sea. Dylan wrote to his friend who had rented it for him: 'This is it, the place, the house, the workroom, the time. Here I am happy and writing.'

In his hut, after a morning spent at the local pub, as his wife, Caitlin, described it, he would 'bang into intensive scribbling, muttering, whispering, intoning, bellowing and juggling of words.' Laugharne is an English-speaking town, whose mayor goes by the ancient title of 'portreeve,' and whose inhabitants distrusted outsiders. 'We used to throw stones at him,' one resident said. 'Why?' the reporter asked. 'Because he came from Swansea.' Swansea is twenty-seven miles away.

So Dylan too was from away. But he loved the place. It was, he wrote, 'the best town, the best house, the only castle, the mapped, measured, inhabited, drained, garaged, townhalled, pubbed and churched, shopped, gulled and estuaried one state of happiness.'

My friend must have thought my new place resembled Dylan's. In some ways it does. But the distance from the sea is greater and there seems to be no danger of my study falling into the sea. True, mine is a place where juggling of words takes place. True, for me 'This is it: the place, the house, the workroom, the time.' Sadly, I doubt I shall ever achieve, as he did, what he called 'the mystery of having been moved by words.'

∽

None of the bookcases in our house stands erect. The floors are all uneven. So we buy what are called 'shims,' wedge-shaped pieces of wood to insert under the bookcases, making them level. Tracy, the frugal carpenter, laughs at our purchase—'You actually paid money for those?' We are embarrassed. People from away do that sort of thing, buy what prudent Mainers acquire from the land or from construction leftovers.

My revenge comes later in the week. Tracy runs out of small pieces of wood, and asks if she can have two of our boughten shims. She blushes. I grin with malicious delight.

∽

The many birds that live in our cove, or visit it, make up for the small number of land birds in our woods. We are going to have to put up attractive feeders to build our bird population. After the first day, even the Maine state bird, a black-capped chickadee, has deserted us. The fucking jays are here no longer.

But at the shore: There are many gulls, families of ducks, and cormorants—here called 'shags,' a native corrected me. I am told shags plunge into the sea at the rate of sixty kilometers an hour. Occasionally I spot a sandpiper. Loons make their august progress across the water from one shore to the other. One day, Tracy identified a mysterious (to me) bird as a plover. I have seen one eagle, gliding toward what I hope is its nest in Rebecca Peterson's trees. I look for nests of any variety wherever I walk, having been told on early-morning radio it is a myth to think that touching a nestling will keep the mother away. But I have never seen one.

Sitting in the sun on the deck, clipboard on my lap, binoculars in hand, I am sometimes stopped cold from writing by all the winged action on the water at the end of the meadow.

At last: a hummingbird in a great hurry stops at the colored sugar water I have put out in a feeder among the new boxes of impatiens on the deck. Perpetually in motion, it drinks as it runs, and leaves in a rush. I wait a long time, not daring to move, but it does not return.

෨

I am told, although I have not seen them, that in some parts of Maine, green stamps, long since gone from city stores, still exist. When you have collected them you take them to what is called, with no theological implication, I am sure, a 'redemption store.'

෨

I tend to lose sight of the unpleasant truths that lie just beyond our blessed acreage. This state is not an Eden for everyone. Thirty-seven percent of the population of Hancock County live below the poverty mark; ten percent are said to be functionally illiterate. The county is rural; its unemployment rate is thirty-one percent higher than it is in the large cities like Portland and Bangor. The high school dropout rate is very high, the number of students going on to college very low. In this week's issue of the *Weekly Packet* there are pictures of the twenty-two June graduates from Stonington–Deer Isle High School. Four signify they are going to the University of Maine at Orono, one to Northeastern University in Boston, a few to the Maritime Academy in Castine; the rest expect 'to be employed.' A number of these specify fishing or construction as their future occupation. Some say they do not know exactly what they will do.

The great curse of the population in these beautiful hills and beside the bays, coves, and rivers is alcoholism. The newspaper reports numerous tickets or arrests each week. A large majority are for drunken driving, or O U I, as they abbreviate it, operating a vehicle while under the influence. The crimes we left behind in Washington—homicides, drug pushing and addiction, break-ins, muggings, beatings, and rapes—do not seem to happen here. Someone says to me: 'Yet.' So, while I feel safe in my house and on the streets, and never bother to lock my car, I am reluctant to drive the very dark roads at night.

ç

I have been looking through a book about the work of the painter Marsden Hartley, who was born in Lewiston, Maine, and died twenty miles from where we now live, in Ellsworth. In his youth he traveled widely, to New Mexico, Paris, Bermuda, Berlin, New Hampshire, New York, unable to find a place to settle. The commentator on his paintings writes: 'No place was his place, each proved as lonely as the last. At the end of his life he learned that man's sole strength is in himself.'

The paintings done in and around Ellsworth are his best. His subjects were drowned fisherman, eroded shells, dead plovers left on the beach after a hurricane. Despairing, desolate, hopeless visions, they reflect his desperate desire for death and oblivion. He wrote, at the end of his life:

> . . . And let men have the sea
> Who want eternity.

Bruce Chatwin (with Paul Theroux) has a new book, *Patagonia Revisited*. Before I read it, I reread *In Patagonia*. Looking at 'the enormity of the desert or the sight of a tiny flower,' Chatwin writes, 'the choice is between the tiny and the vast.' In our landscape there is no such necessary choice. Reach and cove, spruce and small berry bushes, giant rocks and beach pebbles, meadow and narrow, beaten path, all coalesce into one harmonious whole. I cannot separate the small from the vast, the evergreen seedling from the enormous horse chestnut tree that shades part of our lawn.

∽

I go down to the cove, carrying my beach chair, intending to work there. But I find I am restless and want to walk in one direction or the other, exploring the little inlets I haven't seen. I think of T. S. Eliot:

> Teach us to care and not to care
> Teach us to sit still.

Sometimes, when I listen to silence in the early evening on the deck, I imagine I hear the whine of police cars and the sirens of ambulances, the whirring of an overhead helicopter searching out a local miscreant, the honking of impatient home-goers held up on North Carolina Avenue by a slow driver, the shouts of teenagers 'hanging out' in the alley.

When quiet descends again, I know I am away from the distressed city and have conjured up the intrusive noise, perhaps so I can better relish the sensation of silence.

∽

I am invited to a cocktail party at the Sargent House, which stands in the middle of the village. Abby Sargent Neese Kelly is a native who now lives outside Philadelphia during the winter but comes back faithfully to the house her grandfather built, and where she was born, in the summer. Her house is filled with fine possessions of her ancestors, including a 'nurse's chair,' connected to the cradle so that as the nurse rocks, so does the baby.

I meet Abby's cousin, who tells me about our house. It seems it once belonged to her great-aunt, Ella Byard, a 'spinster schoolteacher' who, at the beginning of this century, advertised in the newspaper for a husband. Captain Willis White presented himself, and was accepted. However, he turned out to be a poor choice, being a 'terrible womanizer.' Abby and her cousin were not allowed to visit their aunt in the Captain White House, as it was called even then, without a chaperon. Abby's cousin promises to call on me and acquaint me with stories full of terrible details about the infamous Captain White.

Perhaps we should repaint the mailbox to change the name to the Ella Byard House.

∽

An addition to my store of evidence on the longevity of Maine residents and visitors: Anne Chamberlyn, who is over sixty, tells me she owns six bicycles, some in Washington, some in Maine. Every day she rides about forty miles, wherever she happens to be.

∽

In Ellsworth, where I go once a week for groceries, a well-tanned, slim, elderly man in a yacht club cap engaged me in conversation. We were standing at the magazine rack of a store called Mr. Paperback. I was looking at a book called *Basic Sailing*.

'Do you sail?'

I admitted I was only beginning to learn. I have been out in Peggy Danielson's boat three times and am a late convert to the art of moving across the water by wind and sail, in the direction you wish to travel.

'I am a sailor,' he said, with some pride. 'Have been one all my life. Never had to work at anything, so I sailed, first my father's boat, and now mine.'

I tell him how lucky I think he is.

'Well, I suppose. But now I'm thinking about becoming a writer. What do you think of that?'

'What do you want to write?'

'Stories. I want to write stories. I read that there are thirty-eight plots. I'll pick one, change it around a little, set it on the coast of Maine, and write it. I used to know someone who worked for *The Saturday Evening Post*. I'll send it to him.'

Every time I hear the number of plots there are in the world the amount changes, covering a spread from nine to, now, thirty-eight. I refrain from saying that there are as many plots as there are writers narrating them, that the voice telling the story is what matters, and that I rarely see *The Saturday Evening Post* on the newsstands.

∽

July 4. Today there was a celebratory parade in Blue Hill. Sybil and I drove into town and stood at the edge of the road with a sparse, strung-out collection of L. L. Bean–clad onlookers and impatient children. The parade was touching. The band of the local high school led it off, there was one car carrying a very old army veteran, several groups of Girl and Boy Scouts, three or four naval veterans from World War II (no women, of course, but then, I hadn't volunteered to march), a thin line of young children on their bikes, and, at the very end, a little boy riding a donkey, carrying a small American flag, and wearing a hat that rested on his large ears.

The parade stopped at the first bridge, a member of the band played an agonizingly off-key Taps on his bugle, and a naval lieutenant, senior grade, threw a wreath into the bay. The little girl beside me dropped her ice-cream cone and started to cry. Her father picked her up. With the other onlookers, he started walking with the parade toward the next bridge, where the same ceremony was to be performed. Sybil and I went home, feeling patriotic and chastened by the simplicity and good intentions of it all.

∽

Alone in the house (Sybil has gone to Washington and will not be back until the end of this month), I feel the *extent* of it, the number of rooms I never go into unless there are guests, the number of entrances and exits, the lawn and meadow and woods stretching out in all directions, the deck blacked out at night, the circular driveway, the damp, granite cellar down a flight of rickety steps, the half-foot-sized narrow back stairs. All this I inhabit, alone. It seems too much, it has far too many dark holes and ragged edges. I pull it all in around me, close the blinds, light one lamp, read a book, and wait for it to be time to go to bed.

∽

July 12, 1989: No longer am I burdened by the weight of my years. My new age today, a year later, does not worry me. Alone for most of the day, until the promise of dinner with friends tonight, I went for a swim in the cove, conquering its temperature (sixty degrees) by thinking it was not as cold as I expected it to be.

Nor is this day as painful as I thought it might be. I seem not to have grown older in the year, but more content with whatever age it is I am. I accept the addition, hardly noticing it. There may well be the enduring challenge of the 365 steps up the face of the Temple of the Dwarf at Chichén Itzá, but the certainty that I shall never again climb them no longer disturbs me.

O'Henry's last words are said to have been: 'Turn up the lights—I don't want to go home in the dark.' I've begun to try to turn up the lights on what remains of my life.

Waiting on the deck for Ted, Bob, and Peggy to take me to a birthday dinner, I watch my unknown neighbor bring his sailboat to anchor in the cove, furl and wrap his sails, and stand for a moment in the prow looking out to the reach. The light is dimming, the water flattens out from grey to dark-blue calm, the sun sets, coloring the sky like an obscured klieg light, out of my sight.

Now I shall sail by the ash breeze, standing still on the deck.

Living in this beautiful place, I look forward to the solitude it affords me, and to friends to break it with. At the end of the day I shall welcome them to share my board and my luck. Who knows, I may be entertaining angels.

Unlike Anna Pavlova, I have no immediate use for a swan costume. I am ready to begin the end.

Afterwords

*T*his memoir will make a belated appearance, in the fall of my seventy-third year. There are a few changes and developments that have occurred since I gathered together the memories and events of my seventieth year. True, I will disturb the symmetry of the book, or what Aristotle called one of the essential unities of a literary work. But then . . .

• The lovely campgrounds at Kailuum in the Yucatán no longer figure large in my winter plans. I have stored away my mask, snorkel, and fins in an inaccessible place. Friends Tori Hill (of the Library of Congress Reading Room) and Elizabeth Carl, now the Reverend Elizabeth Carl, ordained priest in the Episcopal Church, visited there last winter. They, and ten other campers, came down with what is referred to, euphemistically, as Montezuma's Revenge. Then Tori contracted hepatitis, and was sick for a long time, although it is not at all certain her illness was linked to that idyllic Mexican coast. Nonetheless, my enthusiasm to return is, perhaps foolishly, diminished. . . .

Still, someday I want to stand at the foot of the Temple of

the Dwarf and watch my new grandchild, born early in 1989, scamper up its forbidding steps. It is only fitting that her parents, lovers as I am of the great sites, have named her Maya.

• Last fall, I read of the death of Mary McCarthy, of cancer, at the age of seventy-seven. I half expected it. She had left Castine at the end of the summer and gone to teach her usual semester at Bard College (the institution she had forgiven after her satire upon it in *The Groves of Academe,* or perhaps it would be more accurate to say it had forgiven her). There she died, quite suddenly. When we met at the Blue Hill farmer's market in the summer of 1989, and she left me with that harsh adverb 'unpleasantly,', I regretted that I had not thought of some conciliatory response. Her grey, much-altered face, so beautiful in her youth and maturity, suggested illness to me. She seemed frail as she turned away from me to inspect the vegetables. I am diminished by her death, having once spent almost a year on her life. We all are.

• The Episcopal congregation in Blue Hill has finally found a churchly home for itself. Last winter it purchased, for a very modest price, a handsome old abandoned Methodist church about ten miles out of the town in North Penobscot, and worked through the winter and spring to make it habitable.

Easter was celebrated there. Land has been donated for a new home in Blue Hill, and money raised to move the building, not an inconsiderable enterprise. The steeple and windows, pews and lighting fixtures must be removed, and then the building *cut in half,* mounted on dollies, and drawn through the narrow streets, the overhead wires suspended as it makes its dichotomistic progress. Everyone hopes the aged structure will survive this arduous journey, that it will not rebel against the violence done to its Methodist walls by the new denomination, and that, *mirabile dictu,* we will celebrate next Easter in the resurrected building.

• An irony: By moving to Maine, I believed I had escaped the violence and threat of the city: murderers, muggers, robbers, drug users and their suppliers, the night noises of sirens and helicopters in pursuit of culprits. I had, but now I discover, to my dismay, that fear and anger, violence and threat, belong to every landscape, inhabit even the flower beds and gardens, country lawns and decks.

Omnipresent hungry cats prevented me from having bird feeders in the city. This spring in Maine I acquired three feeders and set them strategically, under trees, on poles on the lawn, on metal arms from the house. An efficient squad of small red squirrels has managed to climb every rope and chain and pole, from the bottom up and the top down. They approach the feeders by leaping, sliding, and climbing the house shingles. They will not be frightened off by my angry, indeed even hysterical, shouts. True, they respond by dropping from incredible heights to the ground. They take up a stand on a nearby piece of granite and chatter harshly at me, the same ka-ka-ka I heard when, as a little girl in Central Park, I was attacked by a grey relative of the same family, large, stringy, and mad. Squirrels, of whatever size, color, or state of mental health, are my new criminals.

Streams of water directed at them affect them not at all. I have been able to devise no defense; I am at their mercy. At first, I took the feeders indoors, empty of seed, symbols of lost battles and ignominious defeat in the war between nature and me.

Later, I found an unattractive but efficacious way to defeat the little fellows. I greased a pole and placed the feeder, awkwardly, at the top. They never managed to ascend, and there were no nearby trees to drop from. Victory, at last? Not at all.

For part of the summer they ate seed dropped by birds at the foot of the feeder, seemed to be satisfied, and then disappeared. But in the fall we discovered they had been happily engaged in removing much of the cellar insulation in order to provide themselves with a cozy pink nest in an old wood bin.

• Wayward Books now resides in a utilitarian-looking building down a path from our house. Inside it is cozier, housing nine or ten thousand books (we're never sure quite how many), a woodstove with comfortable chairs around it, and copies of book-review sections from around the country and England for browsers to read when they tire of buying. It has done moderately well in its first year. Its greatest virtue, for us, is its proximity to the cove, which, despite my worries, is a place of constantly changing interest.

• *Fine Print,* the handsome quarterly magazine about handmade books, invited me to join its board of contributors and then, two years later, announced suspension of publication, after fifteen years of distinguished production by letterpress printing of its fine issues. I begin to wonder if the name carries its own inevitable albatross.

• Aunt Bet is now 103, bright, cheerful, and quite well, living in her nursing home. Her spirits are good. She is still charming, and lovely to look at. Her eyes are somewhat improved; every evening she reads the newspaper. She still enjoys her nip of brandy.